A Gift for

_____

Presented by

_____

I Wish
I Knew
That
Science

I Wish I Knew That Science

Cool Stuff You Need to Know

Stephanie Schwartz Driver
Rachel Garcia, M.F.S., M.A.T.

Reader's Digest

The Reader's Digest Association, Inc.
New York, NY / Montreal

A READER'S DIGEST BOOK

Copyright © 2012 All rights reserved. Unauthorized reproduction, in any manner, is prohibited.
Reader's Digest is a registered trademark of The Reader's Digest Association, Inc.

PROJECT STAFF
U.S. Editor: Barbara Booth
Contributing Writer: Sara Altshul
Designer: Jennifer Tokarski
Illustrator: Andrew Pinder

READER'S DIGEST TRADE PUBLISHING
Senior Art Director: George McKeon
Editorial Director, Trade Publishing: Neil Wertheimer
Manufacturing Manager: Elizabeth Dinda
Associate Publisher, Trade Publishing: Rosanne McManus
President and Publisher, Trade Publishing: Harold Clarke

Library of Congress Cataloging in Publication Data available upon request.
ISBN 978-1-60652-424-4

Reader's Digest is committed to both the quality of our products and the service we provide
to our customers. We value your comments, so please feel free to contact us:

The Reader's Digest Association, Inc.
Adult Trade Publishing
44 S. Broadway
White Plains, NY 10601

For more Reader's Digest products and information, visit our website:
www.rd.com (in the United States)
www.readersdigest.ca (in Canada)

Printed in the United States of America

1 3 5 7 9 10 8 6 4 2

"The most exciting phrase to hear in science, the one that heralds the most discoveries, is not 'Eureka!' (I found it!) but 'That's funny....'"

—ISAAC ASIMOV

CONTENTS

ELECTROMAGNETIC CIRCUS 65

LIFE AS WE KNOW IT   83

WHAT WE ARE AND HOW WE WORK   103

WHY EARTH LOOKS (AND ACTS) LIKE EARTH   121

INTRODUCTION:
HOW IN THE WORLD...?

Whatever it is you want to know, whatever it is you are wondering about, put it into a question. Then watch and observe; the results will amaze you.

Science is all about that—asking, watching, describing, and testing. Finding patterns that repeat, learning from getting it right, and learning from getting it wrong. Trying it over and over again. Science is everything we know about the universe and everything in it.

How come snow is white and the sky is blue? Why is winter cold and summer hot? Why is night dark and day light? Thousands of years ago people were wondering about the same things you wonder about. And the things science has revealed are pretty amazing and fun to know:

- The sun is big enough to hold 1.4 million Earths. It burns 4 million tons of hydrogen in the time it takes you to say the word hydrogen (no wonder it's so bright that it hurts your eyes!). But there's no need to worry about the sun's running out of fuel—it has enough to continue for another 5.5 billion years.

- In your own body, you produce and destroy 15 million blood cells every second—blood that travels through your 60,000 miles of vessels to deliver oxygen and other things to your 60 trillion cells.

- Do you know why kids have 300 bones in their skeleton but adults have only 206? Or why astronauts grow taller in space (and younger)? Or why the Himalayas, already the tallest mountains in the world, are growing taller every year? These are just the kinds of questions scientists ask all the time.

Every time a science question is answered, there are a dozen new ones. There is no end to science. Because there are so many questions to ask, science was eventually divided into different fields, called disciplines, like physics, chemistry, geology, biology, and so on. But what these scientists do all comes down to the same basic question: people looking through a microscope or up at the sky and asking, "What is going on here?"

This book should give you some of the answers to that never-ending question—and encourage you to think of many, many more!

MATTER MATTERS

Everything we see and touch is matter, and matter is made up of atoms. It turns out that atoms aren't the smallest thing around. For a long time they were considered the tiniest building block, but scientists have discovered even smaller particles—quarks and other subatomic particles—that make up atoms. But it's the behavior of atoms that explains a lot about the world around us. Most atoms do not like to be on their own. They usually gang together with other atoms of the same kind or run into others unlike themselves, and that's where all the fun begins.

ATOMS—THE MAIN BUILDING BLOCKS

The study of what atoms do when they bump into each other is called **chemistry,** and to understand it, first you have to know what atoms are made of and how they are made.

Atoms have a hard, solid core called a **nucleus**. The nucleus is made of positive-charged (+) **protons** and neutral (uncharged) **neutrons**. Orbiting around the nucleus are negatively charged (−) **electrons**. Electrons are about 1,000 times smaller than protons! Atoms always have the same number of electrons as protons, and smaller atoms have the same number of neutrons and protons.

The simplest element, hydrogen, is built out of one postive proton in the nucleus (and it doesn't have a neutron), with one negative electron orbiting that proton.

But hydrogen is only one element, and our world is made up of many different ones. Elements differ from one another because of the numbers of these protons and electrons. Hydrogen is just the simplest. Helium, the "lighter-than-air" gas in floating balloons, has 2 protons and 2 electrons and 2 neutrons. Lithium, a metal often used in fancy batteries, has 3 of each. Oxygen has 8 of each. Sodium, the major element in salt, has 11. Chlorine has 17. Gold, a heavy metal, has 79, and so on.

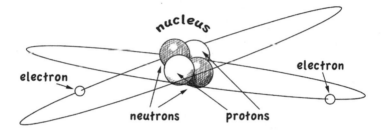

🔬 Discover this!

Atoms are so tiny that scientists today need very specialized microscopes to see them, and those microscopes were not invented until the 1980s. But the idea of atoms has been around for a very long time—since ancient Greece, in fact. In 530 BCE a wise man named Democritus came up with the idea of atoms. The modern understanding of atoms—and of chemistry—didn't come until much later, in the 19th century, when a British teacher and scientist named John Dalton explained much about the way atoms work—without ever seeing one.

There are 118 different elements (as far as we know so far, at least!). Of these, 112 are natural and 5 are synthetically produced in labs. It's when elements combine that things get interesting. For instance, when hydrogen (a gas) and oxygen (also a gas) get together, the oxygen atom prefers to link with two hydrogen atoms and the result is H_2O, or water. Sodium and chlorine join up quite often, especially on our planet, and the result of that, NaCl (sodium chloride), is what we call salt.

Radioactive action

Sometimes the nucleus of an atom will become unstable and break apart. This usually happens with a big nucleus, like uranium, which has 92 protons and electrons and 146 neutrons. When that nucleus breaks apart, it shoots out particles and energy, and that energy is known as **radioactivity.** Sometimes this happens in nature, but sometimes scientists make this happen so they can use radioactivity for good causes—for example, to cure some kinds of cancer—or for dangerous causes, as in atomic bombs.

Liquid, solid, gas—oh, my!

All of the elements at room temperature on the surface of Earth come in one of three states: solid, liquid, or gas. And their state can change when they combine with one another or if you change the temperature. So when your ice cream melts on a hot summer day, it's changing from a solid to a liquid because the steamy hot temperature is affecting it. This kind of change happens all around us. Dry ice, for instance, is carbon dioxide gas that has been chilled down until it turns into a super-cold brick. In other words, it's solidified carbon dioxide.

Water is the only compound that can exist in all three states at room temperature: liquid water, frozen ice, and gaseous steam. But all substances are constantly changing states. For example, plastics and paints "outgas"—that's the name for the way they give off a strong smell as some of their chemical ingredients turn to gas, even though they do not completely change state.

Pure air

The air we breathe is mainly made up of nitrogen, the seventh most abundant element in the universe. Only 21 percent of the atmosphere is oxygen, the gas we think about when we think about breathing.

That oxygen has another very important role in the atmosphere. It is diatomic, meaning it prefers to exist in pairs, or O_2—and it is constantly switching into O_3, or ozone, and back again. Ozone absorbs a lot of the dangerous energy from the sun, acting like a radiation-absorbing shield to protect us. When scientists worry about "the ozone layer," what they are saying is that pollution is interfering with that important layer of gas up there. Weirdly, ozone on the ground is a dangerous pollutant. Good up high and bad down low.

1 H																	2 He
3 Li	4 Be											5 B	6 C	7 N	8 O	9 F	10 Ne
11 Na	12 Mg											13 Al	14 Si	15 P	16 S	17 Cl	18 Ar
19 K	20 Ca	21 Sc	22 Ti	23 V	24 Cr	25 Mn	26 Fe	27 Co	28 Ni	29 Cu	30 Zn	31 Ga	32 Ge	33 As	34 Se	35 Br	36 Kr
37 Rb	38 Sr	39 Y	40 Zr	41 Nb	42 Mo	43 Tc	44 Ru	45 Rh	46 Pd	47 Ag	48 Cd	49 In	50 Sn	51 Sb	52 Te	53 I	54 Xe
55 Cs	56 Ba	57-70	71 Lu	72 Hf	73 Ta	74 W	75 Re	76 Os	77 Ir	78 Pt	79 Au	80 Hg	81 Tl	82 Pb	83 Bi	84 Po	85 At	86 Rn
87 Fr	88 Ra	89-102	103 Lr	104 Rf	105 Db	106 Sg	107 Bh	108 Hs	109 Mt	110 Uun	111 Uuu	112 Uub		114 Uuq				

57 La	58 Ce	59 Pr	60 Nd	61 Pm	62 Sm	63 Eu	64 Gd	65 Tb	66 Dy	67 Ho	68 Er	69 Tm	70 Yb
89 Ac	90 Th	91 Pa	92 U	93 Np	94 Pu	95 Am	96 Cm	97 Bk	98 Cf	99 Es	100 Fm	101 Md	102 No

THE PERIODIC TABLE

There's a chart of all the elements, known as the Periodic Table of the Elements, or just the Periodic Table. The letters on it are the names given to all known elements. They are called atomic symbols, and understanding them is the first step in learning the language of chemistry.

The list of elements is more than a long roll call of characters. It was a Russian professor named Dmitri Mendeleev who figured out a way to organize and understand how the elements all fit together.

Mendeleev lived in the last half of the 1800s, and at the time, scientists had identified only about 60 elements. Mendeleev was a big fan of the card game solitaire. Playing cards inspired him to make a set of cards, one for each element. On each card he wrote everything that was known about each element— mainly how it behaved in the presence of other elements and

how willing it was to react with them. He arranged the atoms by atomic weight.

What emerged was a pattern. Similar elements stacked in the same columns: lithium (Li), sodium (Na), and potassium (K) belonged in the same row, just as beryllium (Be), magnesium (Mg), and calcium (Ca) did. And the pattern not only repeated but also left some tantalizing gaps, suggesting there were elements out there yet to be discovered—which there were!

Mendeleev's winning solitaire hand is basically the Periodic Table of the Elements, and it is still used today as a visual aid to help scientists keep matter in order.

Decoding the Periodic Table

Each element's "card," or box, on the chart is a profile containing all of the key information about it, not unlike a Facebook page.

- First, **atomic symbol**, or code name. Some of them, like H for hydrogen and O for oxygen, make perfect sense. Some are easy to guess, like Ca... Calcium? Or Mg... Maybe magnesium? But others seem to make no sense whatsoever. K for potassium? A little Latin can help with some of them. For instance, the atomic symbol for gold, Au, comes from *aurum,* the Latin word for gold (Aurora was their goddess of the glowing sunrise). Sodium's code name, Na, is another puzzler, until you learn that sodium was called *natrium* in ancient Rome. Potassium's K, by the way, comes from *kalium,* the Nordic word for the element.

- The next item in the profile is the **group**, or column. Columns stack up all the elements that behave similarly when put into the same environment. For example, when dropped in water, group 1's lithium, sodium, and potassium all tend to fizz away.

- Also in the profile is the **period**, describing in ascending order how reactive the element is compared to the other members of its column. This quality describes how easily each type of atom bonds with other atoms. Each element is less reactive than the one on top of it.

- The **atomic number** tells how many protons are in the nucleus, as well as the order in which the elements appear right to left.

- The **atomic weight** gives the element's mass.

ELEMENT + ELEMENT = COMPOUND

Most elements rarely exist on their own in pure form; they prefer to combine with others. When different elements combine, the result is called a **compound.** The atoms of each element in the compound bond together by sharing or exchanging electrons. When atoms combine like this, the results are known as **molecules.** When elements combine to make molecules, they become a new, tight unit, with its own nature. Think about it: Water, H_2O, behaves very differently from either hydrogen or oxygen alone, and it's not easy to split it apart. Hydrogen and oxygen are gases at room temperature, but water is a liquid.

One of the neatest things about chemistry is how atoms always combine in units measured in whole numbers. Water is two hydrogen atoms and one oxygen atom, not two and a third and maybe one and a half. Table salt is one sodium plus one chlorine, period.

All about ice pops

We know that plain old water freezes (and melts) at 32°F, or 0°C. That's the temperature we call "freezing." But if we add something to that water, it will have a different freezing point.

Ice pops are made by adding fruit juice, or sugar and flavoring, to water. (A bit of food coloring is usually also added to make it bright red, green, blue, or whatever fun colors the makers have in mind.) Adding those extra ingredients to the water makes it a solution, meaning that something (the sugar or juice) is dissolved into the water. The more sweetener, the softer the finished product is—as you can imagine, it's much easier to bite off a soft bit of ice pop than it would be to chomp down on a solid block of ice!

Adding sugar, salt, or any other substance to water will lower the water's freezing point. In other words, adding something makes the water harder to freeze or easier to melt. So the ice pop will take longer to freeze than plain water would. By the way, when an ice pop melts, it changes state, from solid (frozen water and sugar or juice) to liquid (sticky, melted water and sugar or juice).

Compounds made up of elements can always be written with the atomic symbol, with a little number next to it indicating how many atoms of that element is in one unit of the compound. So that's why water is also sometimes called H_2O—it is a compound made of two hydrogen atoms and one oxygen atom.

One molecule of hydrochloric acid is HCl, meaning one hydrogen atom to one chlorine (a very potent acid that can eat through metal but also exists in your stomach to help break down food). These are pretty simple compounds, but others can be much more complicated. The recipe for sulfuric acid, also nothing to mess around with, is more complex: H_2SO_4. Two hydrogens, one sulphur, and four oxygens.

Getting to the base of acids

Some acid, like hydrochloric acid, are strong and dangerous. But there are also weak acids, such as the citric acid found in orange juice and the acetic acid in vinegar. Weak acids are every bit as useful as the strong ones. The thing that all acids have in common is that they really want to give up a proton. And acids' counterparts, called bases, are more than anxious to take that proton off any acid's hands. The so-called acid-base reaction is one of the liveliest in nature and in the chemistry lab and is happening all around us all the time. It is one of the most basic reactions there is (pun intended!).

Discover this!

All living things have one element in common: carbon, or C. Its name is from the Latin word *carbo*, meaning charcoal. And it is a good example of how combinations and different states can make what seems like magic happen. Think about it: 20 percent of your body weight is carbon. Carbon exists in more than half of all the known compounds in the universe. When you subject carbon to immense pressure over millions of years, it turns into a crystal-clear sparkling diamond, one of the hardest (and most expensive) substances known. But carbon also makes up graphite, which is what pencil lead is made of. This form of carbon is so soft that it rubs off onto paper.

THE CHEMISTRY BEHIND THE "VOLCANO"

Have you ever tried to make a volcano demonstration? It's fund to see the explosive bubbling.

The chemical reaction between baking soda and vinegar produces a gas called carbon dioxide. If you trap the gas in the bottle, it will "explode" over the top or even pop a cork out of the top. If you are planning to pop a cork, wear safety goggles to protect your eyes. You can even cover the bottle with sand, clay, or some other kind of material that makes it look more like a volcano.

You can easily make the bubbling, but you'll need a bottle to make it explosive. If you do the chemical reaction in a small bowl, you can go slowly and experiment. Try adding the vinegar slowly and watch it bubble. If you add the vinegar faster, will the bubbles grow faster? If you add some soap, what happens then?

Materials

- Baking soda
- Food coloring (optional)
- Dish soap (optional)
- Vinegar
- 1/4 purple cabbage
- Water
- Bowls
- Funnel
- Bottle
- Cork
- Food processor, blender, or knife
  and cutting board
- Strainer
- Measuring cup (optional)
- Tablespoon
- Safety glasses

To produce a dramatic reaction, you will need to use a lot of material. Make sure you do this reaction in the sink, outside, or in a bucket to catch spills.

Procedure

1. Put ¼ cup baking soda in your bowl. For special effects, add food coloring to make it look cool or a few drops of soap to make it even foamier.

2. Add ½ cup vinegar and watch out! If you add more vinegar, what happens?

continued ▶

3. For special effects, try this experiment in a small bottle. You'll need to use a funnel to get the baking soda and then the vinegar inside. Try capping the bottle with a cork. Will it blow?

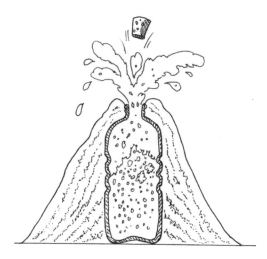

The reaction of baking soda and vinegar is a neutralization reaction. When you mix an acid (vinegar) and a base (baking soda), you create a neutral substance, which is neither an acid nor a base. To show what is acid, what is base, and what is neutral, you can make an indicator with purple cabbage juice.

Procedure

1. Chop up ¼ purple cabbage with about a cup of water. Strain out the cabbage and keep the colored liquid. The liquid will be a bluish or purplish color.

2. Now test your materials. Measure one tablespoon of baking soda into a bowl and add a tablespoon of cabbage juice. Watch what color the juice turns. It should turn bright blue, indicating that you have a base.

3. Next, test your vinegar. Add a few drops of cabbage juice to one tablespoon of vinegar. It should turn pinkish, because vinegar is an acid. You can try your cabbage indicator on other common foods. What happens with orange juice, milk, or soda?

4. Add the pink vinegar to the baking soda. What happens? Did the color change? Is the reaction finished?

5. Keep adding vinegar until the color changes from bright blue to purple. The bubbling will stop when all the acid and base are neutralized. If you keep adding vinegar, will the color turn pink again?

GET A MOVE ON

EVERYTHING THAT MOVES FOLLOWS THE SAME RULES (WELL, JUST ABOUT EVERYTHING).

Everything in the universe moves. In fact, everything is moving all the time, even if we don't notice it. Even now, as you're sitting to read this, you're actually moving. The Earth is moving around the sun, the sun is zooming around the Milky Way—and even the electrons in the atoms that make up your body are busily whizzing around. Sounds like a recipe for chaos and disaster, doesn't it? Luckily, everything—from the atoms to the planets—are following a few basic rules. The study of motion is part of the branch of science called physics, and people have been working on this for thousands and thousands of years.

A long, but not boring, story

The stories of the laws of motion and gravity feature the greatest scientists in history. These were men who noticed things that were very ordinary, even boring, yet still wondered why.

It all started in ancient Babylon 4,000 years ago. Probably with not much else to look at after the lights were out, Babylonians were fascinated with the way the sun and moon and planets moved across the sky. They took notes about what they saw—lots of notes—and started to see patterns that made it possible for them to start predicting things. They learned when Mars would appear over a particular part of the sky, but also, more usefully, when the seasons would change. They made a calendar that was simply based on watching the sky.

It's not all Greek

Jump ahead 1,500 years and a small journey to the west, and there's a bunch of people in Greece looking at the natural world around them and asking all sorts of questions and coming up with some amazing answers. One of them was the Greek philosopher and teacher Aristotle. He told his students that rather than imagining and debating how many different kinds of shells there were on the beach, they should start collecting them, then line them up, then sort them by size and color and shape. It was all about careful observation and looking for patterns. This was the first science class ever, and it took place more than 2,400 years ago.

Aristotle was a great observer. Like everyone before him, he was raised to think the Earth was a huge flat platform with the light show of the heavens streaking above. Then one night he saw a lunar eclipse. He watched the shadow of the Earth creep across the face of a full bright moon as it blocked the light of the sun, and he couldn't help but notice that the shadow was round. From that evidence, he figured out that the Earth must be round, too, not flat as everyone had always assumed.

He also looked at the ships sailing away from the Greek shores and disappearing gradually over the horizon, the uppermost parts of the mast and sails the last things to disappear. It looked to him as if the ships were going downhill.

Based on these two observations, Aristotle realized that the Earth, like the moon and sun, was a huge ball and not a gigantic tabletop. But even Aristotle, one of the greatest philosophers ever, could make mistakes, and his understanding of how the sun and moon and planets moved didn't pass the test. He thought they circled the Earth and that all the rest of the stars in the sky were stuck in the roof of the heavens, never moving, and he figured that the ceiling itself was probably not very far above Saturn.

What propelled the sun and moon and Mercury, Venus, Jupiter, and Saturn (the only planets he could see)? Aristotle suggested there had to be a divine or magical force pushing them along. He called it a "Prime Mover," and for centuries to come, lots of priests and holy men liked that idea. Didn't Apollo's fiery chariot shuttle the sun across the sky in the Greek scheme of things? And angels had wings, reasoned

Christians, so they must be busy pushing the planets through the sky. The reason no one could see them was because angels were invisible.

Aristotle's view would persist for a thousand years. The Earth never moved, and the reason all things fell toward the Earth when you dropped them was because the Earth was the center of the universe. That way of looking at the universe is called **geocentric,** from the Greek words for Earth and center.

ROUND AND ROUND WE GO

Many many years later, in the 1500s, along came a Polish priest and math teacher named Nicholas Copernicus. He lived at a time when people were questioning everything, and he became convinced that Earth was not at the center of the universe but was, instead, just another planet that traveled in a circle around the sun. He reached this revolutionary new understanding by studying measurements and data about the paths of the planets and stars, information that had been collected since the time of the Babylonians. "We revolve around the Sun like any other planet," Copernicus claimed. His ideas were well ahead of his time, and it was more than 100 years before another scientist dared to go against popular opinion and take up the cause.

A guy named Galileo

A generation later an Italian scientist named Galileo dreamed up a new invention called the **telescope**. He used it to carefully observe the heavens, looking at the the Milky Way and the planets Saturn and Venus. He also used it to get more detailed evidence to prove that Copernicus was right. Galileo was a math teacher and star gazer, and he is often called the founder of modern science because of his devotion to experimentation and observation. He once said, "All truths are easy to understand once they are discovered; the point is to discover them."

Galileo made many important discoveries. He was one of the first to say that the reason a cannonball shot through the air (something he would have had the chance to see) and traveled in an arc was due to the forces acting upon it: the first push from the gunpowder toward the target, and then something—gravity—pulling it toward the center of the Earth (not that he called it gravity; the force wasn't named for another 100 years). Why couldn't the same idea explain the orbits of the planets around the sun?

Galileo defended Copernicus's ideas, and he was sentenced to house arrest for the last years of his life for daring to promote the idea that the Earth was not the center of the universe and that there were other mysterious forces at work in the world. The Catholic Church also criticized him, and it wasn't until 1992 that Pope John Paul II admitted that maybe the Church had made a mistake.

Seeing near and far

When Galileo invented the telescope, he brought the heavens down to Earth, and not everyone liked what he saw.

Galileo had heard that a Dutch scientist had created a "viewing tube," but that guy was keeping the details top secret so no one would steal his idea. Right away, Galileo decided to copy him. (They say that imitation is the sincerest form of flattery....) His first telescope was really simple—two lenses, one at either end of a long tube—and it made things look three times bigger than they really were. But with hard work and through trial and error, he eventually ended up with something that enlarged things by 20 times. Very quickly he began to see things no other man or woman had ever observed: He saw that the surface of the moon was covered with mountains and pitted with craters; he saw our galaxy, the Milky Way; and with these and other observations, he realized that the Earth was not the center of the universe.

People who didn't like Galileo's idea blamed the telescope—some rival scientists wouldn't even try to look through it, thinking that it was dangerous. But other scientists were really excited about the idea, including Isaac Newton, who invented an even better telescope 30 years after Galileo's death, using mirrors inside the tube to make it more powerful.

Don't panic, it's miles away

NEWTON'S NOGGIN

The next player in the story is one of the greatest minds of all time—a man who unlocked more secrets of the universe than all the scientists before him combined. In fact, there is not a branch of science or math that did not advance after he looked into it.

His name was Isaac Newton. Born in an English farm village in 1642, he was a scrawny, sickly kid who wasn't really interested in learning and got picked on by the school bully. That school bully also happened to be the top student. Isaac made up his mind to get back at the bully by doing better in school. So he started to study really hard. And even as a boy, he was fascinated with science and inventions—he even invented a mini windmill that was powered by a mouse running on a treadmill.

Newton went on to prove not only that the Earth and all of the planets moved around the sun in elliptical (like a flattened circle) orbits, but he also used the measurements to show that the natural laws governing the motion of the planets united in a simple, elegant formula that explained everything. Everything! The rules not only applied to the Earth and the planets moving around the sun but also to a stone catapulting through the air or an apple falling from a tree.

The book he wrote describing his theories has been called the greatest science book ever written. And everyone agrees. It did have the most boring name, though. It was titled *Principia,* the Latin word for "principles."

The lingo of physics

Sir Isaac Newton came up with three simple laws that explain everything about motion—and by explaining motion, he also explained staying still.

His three laws are basically this:

1. If a thing is moving or at rest, it will keep doing what it's doing unless some other force is applied to it. This is called **inertia.**

2. If a force is applied to something, its speed (and/or its direction) will be changed. This is called **acceleration.** Acceleration is related to mass—the more mass something has, the more force you need to accelerate it.

3. When a force is applied to an object, the object pushes back with the same amount of force. You might hear this said this way: To every action, there is an equal and opposite reaction.

Soccer ball science

You can demonstrate all three of Newton's rules of motion yourself, using just your foot and a soccer ball.

Rule 1. A ball is sitting on the ground waiting for you to kick it. And it will stay there until you do kick it. While it is sitting on the ground, the ball is showing you what **inertia** is.

Rule 2. You hop to it and kick it, connecting with your big toe. The ball blasts away. This shows you Rule 2—you applied force to the ball, and it began moving.

Rule 3. Your toe hurts. You kicked the ball, and in its own way, the ball kicked back when it met your force (the kick) with its own (its stillness, or inertia).

THE FALLING APPLE

The most famous story about Newton tells of him seeing an apple falling to the ground and wondering why it fell straight down. Inspired by that simple event, he came up with the concept of gravity (and by extension, the calculations that would lead to his invention of the branch of math called calculus).

Newton said there was a force called gravity, as Galileo had described, that affected not only large objects, like planets, but also the things on Earth, like apples. This was a big change. Generally, scientists before Newton believed that there was one set of rules for the heavens and another set of rules for the Earth. But as Newton figured it, gravity is a relationship between any two objects (the Earth and the moon, or even the Earth and an apple falling from a tree) that takes into account the distance between the two objects and their mass (basically, the amount of matter an object contains).

Grateful for gravity

Picture the moon orbiting the Earth. There are really two forces at work: inertia (the moon's moving and it's going to keep moving) and gravity (it is also being pulled directly to the center of the Earth because the Earth is the bigger player in the gravity game). If gravity had an off switch and you hit it, the moon would immediately take off on its own path, finding its own orbit around the sun. Or picture yourself zooming over the highs and lows of your favorite roller coaster—it's only thanks to the gravitational attraction of the Earth that you stay in your seat instead of flying into outer space (OK, maybe the seatbelts deserve a little credit, too).

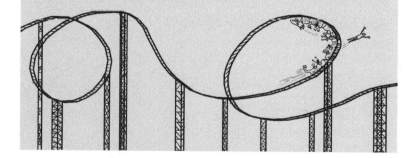

IT'S ALL RELATIVE

Newton came up with his idea of gravity in the 1680s, and for centuries nobody messed with it. But he once famously said, "If I have seen further than others, it is by standing upon the shoulders of giants. To myself I am only a child playing on the beach, while vast oceans of truth lie undiscovered before me." Very poetically put. But it was only a matter of time before someone climbed up on *his* shoulders.

That was Albert Einstein, the most famous scientist of the 20th century. In Einstein's complicated view of the world, which sounds a lot like science fiction but is actually great science, Newton's rules of motion work just fine for most of what happens around us. But when it comes to objects that are moving really, really fast—like at the speed of light, the fastest thing in the universe—all the rules change.

When something goes that fast, Einstein thought, time actually slows down. And when something does get to that speed, it no longer has mass—it's just energy. This is where Einstein's famous formula, $E=MC^2$, comes from. Energy equals mass (times a constant measure, the speed of light, which scientists call "C," multiplied by itself).

Put simply, energy and matter are two forms of the same thing, even though they don't seem to have that much in common at first, kind of like water and ice cubes. That's why Einstein's ideas are known as the theory of relativity: Time and space and stuff are all kind of relatives.

THE FRICTION FACTOR

So if everything is moving all the time, what makes things slow down or stop? Well, that's where friction comes in, at least for solid objects like balls, or cars, or kids, or even airplanes. (There's also a kind of friction with liquids, but that's another story....)

Friction is also a force, and it acts in the opposite direction to movement. It's the force that stops anything that wants to slide. So when you kick the soccer ball and it rolls down the field, it slows down and eventually stops because of the friction between the ball and the field surface.

Some surfaces make more friction and some make less. A smooth surface creates less friction than a rough one—that's why a bowling ball goes so easily on an oiled lane but your soccer ball doesn't zoom on a rough soccer field. That's also why a car will skid when it tries to stop on a wet road: The water on the road reduces the friction between the road and the tires. A handy lesson here—you can reduce friction between solid objects by adding something that makes the surfaces slide better when they meet, like the oil does in a car engine or the wax does on skis.

But speaking of water, friction happens only with solid objects, so water and air do not create friction. Instead, they create resistance to motion by colliding with the solid object. When you swim, you're pushing through the water, basically colliding with trillions of water molecules, and when a plane flies through the air, it's colliding with trillions of air molecules.

This all makes it sound like friction is annoying and a waste of...well, energy. But actually, we rely on friction all the time. Without friction that soccer ball you just kicked would end up rolling across the country, cars would spin their wheels and never get anywhere, and the nails that hold your home together would just fall out of the wood.

HOW DO AIRPLANES FLY?

For hundreds of years everyone agreed about gravity. The apple fell in front of Newton (thankfully not on his head), the moon stays in orbit around the Earth, and you stay on land rather than floating away. That's gravity doing its job. But—and this is a big one—airplanes, which are much larger than apples, can fly. In fact, an empty passenger airplane can weigh as much as 270,000 pounds, and that's before you put the people and the luggage in it. So where's gravity in this?

Well, it turns out that gravity isn't the only force out there. There are also the four forces that get airplanes in the air and keep them moving forward, but not too fast. These forces are weight, lift, thrust, and drag.

Weight is an easy one. Every time you step on the scale, you measure your weight, which is gravity forcing down on you. Airplanes normally weigh quite a lot. So how do they get all that weight off the ground?

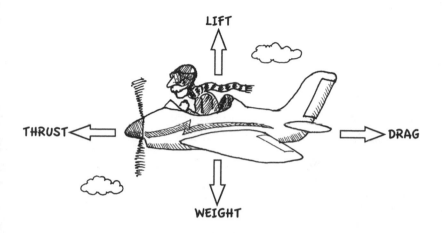

LIFT

THRUST

DRAG

WEIGHT

Airplanes rely on their specially-shaped wings and the force called lift to get them off the ground and keep them in the air. First, an airplane does have strong engines. As the plane accelerates along the runway, getting ready to take off, the airplane's wings cut through the air, splitting the air in two directions: Some goes up and over the top of the wings, and some goes underneath the wings. The wings are shaped so that they're curved on top and flat on the bottom, and so the air moving over the top of the wings has farther to go than the air underneath. That also makes the air above the wing go faster than the air moving underneath. The result is that the force of the air pressure above the wings is lower than the air pressure under the wing. Move fast enough (and airplanes move very fast) and eventually the higher pressure under the wings creates a force that *lifts* the wings—and also the plane that they're attached to. *Phew!*

Now, that explains how the plane gets up into the air, but once it's up there, it has to keep moving somehow. That's where a force called thrust comes in. Thrust is the force that pulls the airplane through the air, and it's created by the propeller or the jet engines on the plane. There is an opposite force to thrust—that's drag. And drag *is* a drag—it's the force that resists the movement of the plane. You can feel drag yourself if you stick your hands (carefully) out of the window of a moving car. Airplane engineers and designers work hard to reduce drag by making the shape of their plane "aerodynamic," giving the drag less surface to push on.

The problem with black holes

Black holes are gravity gone crazy and out of control. They have the most gravitational pull of anything—they suck everything in, and nothing ever escapes, not even light.

A black hole is what is left when a gigantic star—at least 30 times bigger than the sun—dies in outer space (no, your backpack isn't a black hole, even though your homework keeps disappearing into it!). When huge stars run out of fuel, they explode and collapse into themselves, sucking everything around them in.

There are black holes throughout outer space. Scientists even think there's one in the middle of the Milky Way, our galaxy, and they've noticed many others here and there. Astronomers know where they are because they see stuff in space acting strangely, as if there was something big nearby exerting gravity, but there's nothing they can see that might be exerting the force.

DEMONSTRATING NEWTON'S LAW OF INERTIA WITH A MARBLE IN A PIE PAN

Materials

- Disposable aluminum pie pan
- Marble
- Scissors

Newton's first law is called the Law of Inertia. One part of the law states that an object at rest remains at rest unless acted on by an outside force. This statement is not surprising. If you put a marble in a pie pan, the marble won't move at all unless you push it.

The other part of the Law of Inertia is much less obvious. It states that an object in motion continues at the same speed in a straight line unless acted upon by an outside force. If you spent your life in outer space you would make

continued ➤

this observation all the time. However, we usually notice that objects in motion do slow down, and we don't realize that a frictional force is what is changing their motion. Friction happens when molecules get near each other. Even air will cause friction and slow down moving objects.

Although we don't live in outer space, we can demonstrate the second part of the law of inertia by removing a frictional force.

Procedure

1. Obtain a disposable aluminum pie pan. This project is a good opportunity to suggest that your parents need to buy a pie.

2. Cut out one quarter of the pie pan (see diagram at right) and discard it.

3. Place your pie pan on a flat surface. If you place it on a sloped surface, you will only see the effect of gravity on your marble and not observe inertia.

4. Put your marble at one edge. It should not move unless you give it a push. Imagine rolling the marble all the way around the pan to where it is cut out. Every time the marble tries to go in one direction, it is pushed in another by the edge of the circular pie pan by frictional forces. The pie pan continually pushes the marble in a circular path rather than a straight line. Predict what happens if the edge of the pie pan (frictional force) is missing.

Will the marble **(A)** complete the circle with the pie pan missing?

Will the marble **(B)** shoot off in a straight line tangent to the pie pan?

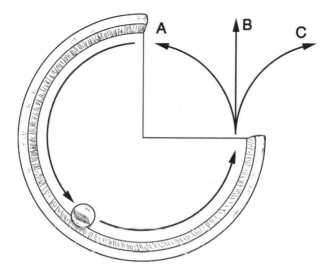

Will the marble **(C)** shoot away from the pie pan in a different direction than it was headed before?

When and where will the marble stop moving?

5. Now give your marble a little push to get it started rolling around and watch what direction it goes when it comes out.

If your marble looks like it completed the circle **(A)** or shoots sideways **(C)** or backward, that is due to gravitational forces—your pie pan is not on a flat surface or you had a problem cutting your pan. If the marble went out in a straight line **(B)**, you have illustrated the Law of Inertia. An object in motion will continue moving in the same direction unless acted on by an outside force. You removed frictional force by removing the edge of the pie pan, and so the marble continued in the same direction it was going. The line it went off in is called the **tangent.**

CATCH A WAVE

When you think about a wave, you may think of holding up your hand and waving at somebody to say hello or maybe good-bye. When you wave your hand, it moves the air a little bit. The motion of your hand creates a disturbance in the air.

There are waves of all types everywhere in our universe. If you throw a rock into a glass-smooth lake or strum a perfectly tuned set of steel strings on an electric guitar—in other words, if you create a disturbance—then waves will launch off, taking that energy and running with it, delivering it to some other place. A ripple of lake water radiates out and laps the shore, or a line of music comes through an electric guitar's amplifier, rips through the air, and rattles your eardrums!

WHAT IS A WAVE?

The basic wave has a familiar shape—an S on its side, going on and on. The high point of the crest is the **peak;** the low point is the **trough.** Waves are measured in three ways:

The **wavelength** is the distance from one peak to the next.

The **amplitude** is the total height of the wave, from the bottom of the trough to the tip of the peak.

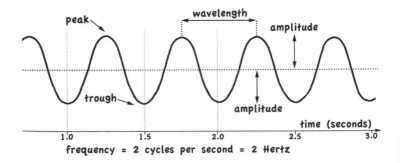

And the **frequency** is how many waves are passing a fixed point per second.

Were you ever part of "the wave" at a sports stadium? You stand up and then sit down, and the person next to you stands up slightly after you and sits down slightly after you, and so on down the row. You don't move away from your seat; you just stand up and sit down. Likewise, when you throw a rock in a lake, the water doesn't move away from where it started—only the energy travels, not the material itself.

Usually waves travel through a medium (air, water, the Earth), delivering energy from wherever they started to another place, without changing or damaging whatever they're traveling through. When a sound wave travels through air, only the energy of the wave reaches your ear. (The air itself moving would be wind, not sound.) If an ocean wave goes under a piece of floating wood or a buoy, the object will bob up and down but not really move side to side away from its spot.

> ### 🔬 Discover this!
>
> Next time you do "the wave" with a group of people, think about this. The amplitude of your wave is just how high your fingertips are (the top of the peak) compared to where you're sitting (the trough, or low point).

Wave wonders

In the ocean, there are the waves we like to play in on the beach. Then there are the terrifying waves generated by a much more explosive disruption, like an undersea earthquake, a force of nature that can release as much energy as a hundred atomic bombs. The waves sent off to transfer that kind of energy can grow to towering heights and move 500 miles an hour, as fast as a jet airplane. They are called **tsunamis**.

A **shock wave** is a disturbance that moves so fast through its medium that the medium cannot handle it, so it ends up crashing into itself because it cannot get out of its own way. When a jet airplane travels faster than the speed of sound, for instance, the waves it gives off cause the air to crash into itself, and the result is a very loud boom. The impact from an explosion is the same way. The waves radiate so fast through the air that they force the air to crash into itself, quite noisily.

Seismic waves are waves that travel through the Earth. They are usually caused when huge pieces of the Earth's crust, sometimes the size of a whole continent, grind past each other or when a volcano erupts violently. Seismic waves are measured with a seismometer, and seismographs draw the squiggly lines showing how strong an earthquake is. The strength of seismic waves is measured from 1 (weak) to 10 (violently strong) on a Richter Scale, named after Charles Richter, a scientist at the California Institute of Technology (Cal Tech) in the early part of the 1900s. Every increase of one point on the scale means it's 10 times as strong as the prior number, so a 6-point quake is 10 times as strong as a 5-point quake. No "10" has ever been recorded.

WAVES FROM THE SUN

The sun is the source of many waves. What we call light is only a narrow band of frequencies from the full menu of waves coming to Earth from our nearest star. X-rays, micro-waves, and radio waves are all produced by the sun. Some get through the atmosphere; others don't.

Light travels at 186,000 miles per second, but it changes its speed when it enters a different medium, like the Earth's atmosphere. The change in speed makes each wavelength bend a little differently, or refract, splitting white light into all of its component parts, which is called the **spectrum.** It is what gives our world its colors, including red sunsets and golden dawns.

Light waves have frequency, amplitude, and wavelengths, and they have peaks and troughs, just like other waves. The vari-ous colors of visible light have different wavelengths. (Regular "white" light, including sunlight, is actually a combination of several colors of light together.) Red has the longest wavelength, or distance between each peak of the light wave, and violet has the shortest. Infrared means "below red," and this invisible "light" has even longer wavelengths than regular red; ultraviolet is "beyond violet" and has even shorter wavelengths.

Rainbows

The scientist Isaac Newton explained how light creates a rainbow when it passes through a prism, or triangular-shaped piece of glass. The glass is the medium that causes the light to refract. Rainbows are formed the same way. It is as if a big storm is acting like a giant prism. Light and water interact to put on a fantastic natural light show. As light passes through each raindrop, it is refracted. We see the wide bands of a rainbow because we only see one color from each raindrop. We see the red from the raindrops higher in the sky because the red wavelength is coming out at the right angle to be seen from our vantage point. Lower raindrops break the light into waves at a different angle, showing us the various colors of the rainbow in their familiar order.

SOUND WAVES

Traveling in the air, sound waves are relative slowpokes, taking about five whole seconds to cover a mile. Light, on the other hand, is much quicker. That is why you see lightning before we hear it (unless it is right on top of you!) and why you can see fireworks explode before you hear their boom.

But sound waves are quirky. The thicker the medium they are traveling through, the faster they move. (You'd think it would be the opposite. When you walk through thick mud, it's harder to move, right? Sound waves really are quirky.) Under water, for example, sound travels four times as fast as it does in the air. It also travels faster through an iron or steel beam than through air (17 times as fast), which is how somebody can feel a train coming a mile away by touching the track. (Take our word for it. Don't try this on your own.) The vibration of the train rumbling down the track is transmitted through the iron rail much more quickly than the sound of it can travel through the air to the person's ears.

Sound wave frequencies are measured in **hertz,** abbreviated Hz, named after German physicist Heinrich Hertz. Humans can hear sounds between about 20 Hz and 20,000 Hz.

Get in tune

Stringed instruments, like guitars and violins (and even pianos), work by allowing their strings to vibrate at certain frequencies. The frequency is controlled first by the length of each string and then by the player's finger on the neck. Longer, looser strings produce low notes, while shorter, tighter strings produce higher tones.

When you put your finger on the fret of a guitar or at the right place on a violin's neck, the string becomes shorter and makes a higher note when plucked or bowed.

Interestingly, putting your finger halfway down a string will produce a note exactly one octave higher than the original string did, like sounding a high C on a middle C string. This is because the frequency is doubled if the string is made half as long.

When a guitar is out of tune, two or more of its strings are producing sound waves in conflicting patterns. (The same thing happens if two trumpets play slightly off-key from each other.) Their sound waves clash, and like synchronized swimmers who aren't quite in sync, they combine in a way that isn't harmonious and smooth. One distracts from the other. In comparison, two guitar strings that are in tune will produce two sound waves that combine into one pleasant-sounding sound wave, reaching your ear as a "good" sound.

Sometimes two different sounds can cancel each other out entirely by moving exactly opposite from each other. This is called **destructive interference** of the waves. That's how "noise-canceling" headphones work: The headphones emit sound whose wave is exactly opposite to the noise's wave, and the combined wave is totally flat, providing silence. (It's the same principle that allows you to walk slowly down an "up" escalator and stay on the same step the whole time. Your movement down the stairs and the escalator's movement upward at the same pace cancel each other out, and you don't move forward/down or backward/up.)

Stretching sound

Why does the sound of a train rushing past or a police car's siren going by seem to change pitch while it's moving? The answer is called the **Doppler effect:** When the vehicle is coming toward you, the sound waves are compressed or squished together more and more, and the pitch gets higher. Then, when it passes you and goes away, the sound waves get stretched out, making the noise sound lower and lower. The frequency of the sound waves gets higher and then lower, making the sound higher and then lower, too.

A whale of a noise

Because sound travels so much faster in water and can go much farther, whales are able to communicate with each other over very long distances—20 miles (30 km) or more—by making low-frequency sounds. Male humpback whales are known for their "songs," which may go on for a full day. This communication is especially helpful to them during mating season. These songs are so low (such low frequency) that humans cannot hear some of them at all.

RADIO WAVES

All around us, traveling at the speed of light, are electromagnetic waves carrying all kinds of information. These "radio waves" send and receive cell phone calls, long-distance landline phone calls, broadcast TV, and of course radio broadcasts. (Local landline phone calls and cable TV are transmitted through electric cables or glass fiber-optic cables, not through the air.) These waves are part of the light spectrum but have much longer wavelengths (often miles long).

Radio waves have a long history. Heinrich Hertz discovered them in 1887. Soon after, Guglielmo Marconi invented the wireless telegraph in 1896 to send Morse code messages over several miles. Marconi was able to send the first wireless signals across the English Channel in 1899, and his invention paved the way a few years later for the invention of the radio.

How do cell phones make calls?

Cell phones, or mobile phones, use radio waves to make and receive calls. Your phone sends out a signal to an antenna on a cell tower that's a few miles away, and then a computer routes those calls either to another cell tower (for calling another cell phone) or to regular telephone lines (for calling a landline). If one cell tower is too busy or has a power outage, the signal gets routed to another tower. All of this coming and going happens in just a few seconds!

Outerspace radio waves

Astronomers learn a lot about space by using radio telescopes, which are large dish-shaped telescopes about 10 times the size of a satellite TV dish. In 1932 an engineer named Karl Jansky, who was studying lightning interference for Bell Telephone Laboratories in New Jersey, noticed radio waves coming from space—and that was the beginning of radio astronomy. These telescopes receive radio waves (longer waves than visible light has, so we can't actually see them). Scientists using them have discovered quasars, pulsars, and other distant bodies far from Earth. Sometimes several small dishes are combined into a telescope array to "see" comets and other distant bodies more clearly.

On your radio

When music plays on the radio or the announcer speaks into a microphone, the music or speech is converted into electrical signals. These signals change a carrier wave, a special radio wave, in a certain way. This change is called **modulation**. AM (amplitude modulation) radio means that the amplitude of the carrier wave is changed—the amount it goes up and down. In FM (frequency modulation) radio the frequency is changed but the amplitude stays the same—in other words, the vibrations per second change, but not the height of the wave. FM radio transmissions have less problem with interference than AM ones do.

On your radar

Ships and airport traffic controllers use radar every day to keep track of other ships or airplanes. Radar's name comes from **RA**dio **D**etection **A**nd **R**anging. It lets the user detect objects by bouncing radio waves off the objects and listening for the echoes. These are displayed on a screen, and the time it takes each echo to return tells the crew the distance of each object. (That's how bats know how far an object is—they use radar, too!) Radar also helps weather forecasters make more accurate predictions, so that you'll know whether you need an umbrella tomorrow, for example.

Cloaks of invisibility

Some modern aircraft have been designed to be almost undetectable by radar, which "sees" an object by bouncing sound waves off it and noting how soon those waves come back to the radar and at what angle. A military plane, like the F-22 Raptor or the F-35 Joint Strike Fighter, needs to fly to a target area and back without being detected by the enemy. Therefore, its design is made of flat surfaces and sharp edges to allow radar signals to bounce back in a way that makes it invisible or just appears on radar screens like a small point instead of a large plane. Some stealth technology uses materials that absorb radar signals rather than allowing them to bounce off at all. Aircraft using either type of stealth technology will look like a small bird instead of a large jet, or be hard to detect at all!

EXPERIMENT

MUSICAL GLASSES

When you sing, vibrations cross your vocal chords and generate sound waves. The length of the wave is related to the frequency or how often your vocal chords vibrate. Frequency is a fancy word for pitch—how high or low the sound is. Men usually have deeper voices than women do because they have longer and thicker vocal chords to vibrate the sound. Boys have higher voices than men because their vocal chords have not finished growing. The sound from many instruments, such as organ pipes and flutes, depends on the length of the column of air that's vibrating.

In this experiment you will make your own simple instrument that demonstrates the relationship between pitch and the length of the column.

Materials

- 4–6 glasses
- Water
- Chopsticks or other wooden sticks
- Optional: food coloring; other liquids; solids, such as sand or rice; plastic bottles

Procedure

1. Choose four to six matching glasses. Leave one empty and add different amounts of water to the others. Arrange them in a row, from most empty to most full.

continued ➤

2. Strike each glass with your stick and listen to the sound. You'll find that the pitch changes depending on how much water is in the glass. What pattern do you notice?

3. You can experiment by adding water until you find a good spread of tones. You can even tune your glasses to match a real musical instrument! For fun, add some food coloring to make your instrument more artistic.

4. Try playing a few songs. Challenge yourself by mixing the order of the glasses. Can you remember which sound comes from which glass?

More things to investigate

Are there pitches that sound good together? Try striking two or more glasses at the same time to make chords.

Will your instrument sound different on different surfaces? If your glasses are on the kitchen counter, try moving them to the floor or to a wooden table or bring them outside.

Do all liquids produce the same sound? Try filling a glass with another liquid, such as juice, soda, salt water, or oil and comparing it to the water-filled glass.

What if you filled your glasses with a solid? Try filling them with sand, rice, oatmeal, or marbles and compare them with the water-filled glasses.

What if you covered the glass? Would it sound the same? Test this idea by covering a glass with plastic wrap or aluminum foil and compare it to a glass with the same amount of water but no cover.

What if you didn't use glass? Could you make a musical instrument like this with plastic glasses or plastic bottles?

Try tapping the glass very gently and then a bit more strongly. What differences do you notice? The sound you get when you tap the glasses comes from the vibrations you create. When you hit the glass lightly, the vibrations are smaller than when you tap it a bit more sharply.

If you're a musician, try playing your musical glasses as an accompaniment to the musical instrument of your choice. Many string instruments are pitched in a similar way to the musical glasses. Compare a guitar to the musical glasses. With a guitar, the shorter the string, the higher the pitch. When you put your finger on the fret, you're shortening the string. Which glass plays the higher sound—the one with the most water or the one with the least?

ELECTROMAGNETIC CIRCUS

You might have gotten a taste of non-electric living during a power outage or while camping out—there's no TV or computer, no heat or hot food unless you build a fire, and no cold foods or drinks, either! During a campout it's fun to rediscover non-electric living, but it's also great to get back to normal afterward. We can barely imagine life for a few hours without electricity, but it's only been a few hundred years since scientists understood this concept.

WHAT IS ELECTRICITY, ANYWAY?

Everything is made up of atoms—we talked about that in chapter 1—and even electricity comes from atoms. Remember, in each atom, negatively charged electrons orbit around a positively charged nucleus. Those positive and negative charges attract to hold the parts of the atom together. But sometimes something causes an electron to break loose from an atom, and its movement, if it is controlled, creates a current of electricity. And with the right technology, which can be as simple as a bit of copper wire or as complex as the power grid for a whole city, that electricity can be used to do fantastic things. (Another way to look at it is to say that electricity is the flow of electrons, or the flow of electric charge, in a circuit.) If you control this energy, you can use it to power lightbulbs and appliances and hospitals—but it takes the energy of billions of billions of electrons to power even a tiny battery-powered toy car!

Conducting electricity

Some atoms give up their electrons more easily than others. The elements whose atoms give up their electrons easily are grouped as the metals. And substances that give up their electrons easily are good conductors of electricity. Copper is one of the best **conductors**. It allows electrons to jump across its surface easily, moving the electrons along, which is why it is the best metal to use in power cords. Other materials, like rubber and cloth, are bad conductors of electricity (they're called insulators). This is why copper wires are wrapped in rubber—that way, the electricity stays in the power cord and doesn't touch your hand, or the carpet in the TV room, or anything else that it could damage.

It's toast!

Toasters are a good example of the conduction of electricity in action. First you push the lever down to make the toast go down. That lowers a spring-loaded rack that the bread sits on. The lever also turns on the heating elements—these are wires with no insulation on them, so the heat generated by the electricity can escape easily—and the heat toasts the bread. The electricity coming into the toaster has been changed into heat energy, cooking your bread for you. When the toast is ready, a timer in the toaster electronically signals a magnet that attracts a catch, releasing the rack. That lets the rack pop up with a perfectly browned piece of toast! Electric kettles and hair dryers also convert electricity directly into heat.

Current thinking: AC or DC?

An electrical **current** is the flow of electrons from one place to another. Current can be either direct or alternating. This is what the initials DC and AC stand for: direct current and alternating current.

An example of **direct current** is something powered by a battery, such as a flashlight, or through an adaptor, like your computer. The power goes from the battery or through the adaptor to the light or computer but doesn't keep going.

Alternating current, or AC, is what powers most electrical things in our homes. Anything that uses a power cord plugged into the wall is using AC (unless it has an adaptor). The circuit begins at the power station or somewhere else outside of your home, goes through the electrical outlet on the wall, and then into the power cord to the lamp, for example. But the circuit, like a big circle, is completed because the current almost instantly reverses direction, going from the lamp back to the outlet. Then it goes back and forth again. (The word *circuit* basically means circle.) A switch, the kind we have on the walls to turn lights on and off or on appliances or other electronics, breaks the circuit so that energy does not flow the rest of the way around. This interruption causes the power to cut out, turning off the light or other appliance.

SWITCHING IT ON

So electricity comes from sloshing electrons. But how do you get enough electrons to power not just a television but a whole town? That's easy. Electricity comes from power plants—everyone knows that. But how does that work?

At the heart of a power plant is a generator—a machine that uses a magnet to push electrons down a wire. But something needs to power that generator magnet.

Some generators in power plants rely on water power from dams. The first power plant ever, built in 1895, used Niagara Falls to get it going.

When people talk about saving energy, they usually mean using less electricity and less gasoline. We do get a lot of our power from those sources, but there are other important sources of power out there. Solar power (from the sun), hydroelectric power (from moving water), wind power, and even geothermal power (from the Earth's warmth) add to energy availability. Others can use nuclear energy, or steam from burning coal, or wind power to get going. There is even tidal power.

Solar power

All living plants take up energy from the sun and depend on this daily dose of solar power to stay alive and grow. But we can also capture some of that solar energy for later use. Solar cells, which absorb some sunlight and convert it into electrical signals, can be combined to form solar panels. Some homeowners now have solar panels on their roof to collect solar energy to help power the home.

🔬 Discover this!

Many solar-powered vehicles have been built in the last several years. The Helios solar-powered flying wing has a wingspan of 247 feet (75 meters), wider than the wingspan of a Boeing 747 airplane. This "wing" is remote-controlled. NASA has even built an aircraft that's entirely powered by solar energy.

Water and wind power

Water turbines and wind turbines can convert the force of water and air into electricity. To get hydroelectric power, water is usually held back by a dam and then released to rush over the blades of a turbine, like a big paddlewheel on a riverboat. Wind turbines allow air to spin their blades—like a pinwheel that you'd blow on to spin its little plastic blades—and the turbine converts that energy into electricity. (Wind turbines are often called windmills, but since they don't all grind corn or do any other milling, they're not all technically windmills.) Waterwheels were used as early as 2,000 years ago to grind corn, but water turbines weren't used for generating electricity until the late 1800s.

Bring on the batteries

Batteries are self-contained generators that let us power portable things, from flashlights and portable music players to cars and complex medical devices. like pacemakers. These sources of direct current (DC) use stored energy to deliver power only when needed.

One early type of battery, the Leclanché cell, was made by using a glass jar to contain a mix of chemicals, with a wire going from each of the two chambers. The chemicals reacted with each other, and the wire carried out the little bit of electricity that this reaction caused. Modern batteries are similar but are housed in metal, not glass— much safer! Some chemicals in batteries are very dangerous.

Discover this!

The most spectacular form of electricity is lightning, which people in ancient times thought was the work of angry gods. Today we understand that an electric charge builds up in clouds as bits of ice and water crash around up there. After a while the negative charge in the cloud is attracted by a more positively charged area, either from cloud to cloud or cloud to ground.

Remember, lightning is very dangerous. The wiring in a house holds only 20 or 30 amps, but a single lightning strike can carry a current that measures as much as 30,000 amps!

HAIR-RAISING FUN

The next time you take off a sweater, turn off all the lights first and then watch as you pull it off. You might see lots of tiny little sparks of lightning crackling all around your clothes and even from your hair. This is another form of electricity called **static electricity.** It's just a bunch of runaway electrons looking for a new place to roost. Static electricity is also what sticks an air-filled balloon to a wall after you rub it on your hair for a few seconds.

When scientists first started to study these sparks back in the 1600s, they used to generate the sparks by rubbing amber (you know, the ancient hardened tree sap that captured the insects used to make dinosaurs in Jurassic Park). Amber makes a lot of static. So when it came time to give these sparks a name, they once again went back to the ancients for inspiration. Electron meant "amber" in Greek.

MAGNETS ARE ATTRACTIVE

Talk about natural magnetism. A magnet is any substance that can attract or repel iron. It may be naturally magnetic, or it may have been magnetized by another magnet or by some other magnetic field. Some metals, like nickel and iron, can be made magnetic for only a short time, while some metal mixes (known as alloys) will stay magnetic forever. Magnets have poles—north and south—just like Earth does. A north pole charge attracts the south pole of another magnet. (The old rule that "opposites attract" refers to magnets!) Like poles repel each other, and opposites attract.

Magnetism is electricity's inseparable cousin. A British scientist, Michael Faraday, figured this out in the 1830s. He dropped out of school when he was 13 and got an apprenticeship at a book bindery. He started to read and became entranced by experiments in science. He started sneaking into lectures and soon started devising his own experiments. Faraday became convinced by his own gut feeling that electricity and magnetism were actually the same force at

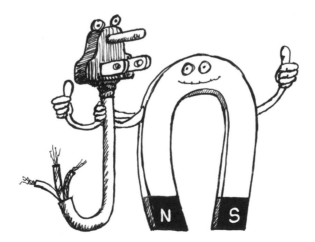

work, and he proved it by creating the world's first electrical generator using magnets. After Faraday's work the world of science invented a new term—**electromagnetism**—which we still use today.

When you run an electric current through a wire, you create a magnetic field. The wire itself doesn't become magnetic, and the magnetic field disappears as soon as you stop the electric current. The greater the current of electricity flowing through the wire, the stronger the electromagnetism becomes. Electromagnets are used in many ways, as the basis for electric motors and generators, and to run the telephones and doorbells in your house.

Push and pull

Electromagnetism's magnetic pull can be very strong, making them good for heavy lifting. Giant magnets are what allow Maglev trains to zoom along at great speeds—much faster than race cars. Their name comes from *Magnetic Levitation*.

This isn't the kind of levitation magicians claim to perform—we're only talking about raising the train a little amount. But these trains do float above the track, traveling friction-free from town to town. They often have wheels as well, because the levitation works only at higher speeds. Maglev trains use magnetism in two ways. A magnet in the train repels the magnets in the track. These trains also take advantage of the fact that magnets attract and repel: Causing the poles to change back and forth from north to south moves the train along the track. The fastest Maglev train, in Japan, travels at over 300 mph (500 km/h)—much faster than regular trains and almost as fast as airplanes! And despite their high speed, they use only about half as much energy as airplanes do for the same distance.

Magnetic munchies

You might not see paper clips clinging to the side of the microwave oven, but a powerful magnet is at the heart of this machine. A "magnetron" inside uses a magnet to convert electricity into invisible microwaves. Those waves are sent toward a fan at the top of the microwave. The fan acts as a propeller to send the microwaves out in a scattered pattern. Without the fan's actions, and without using a rotating plate or hand turning the food occasionally, the microwaves would all go straight to one area in the oven and the food would be burned in one place and raw in another. Yuck! The microwaves make molecules of water in the food vibrate quickly, warming the food up. In many cases, food cooks much more quickly in a microwave than in a regular oven.

Magnetism magic

Ever see someone at the beach or the park using a metal detector? This funny-looking device, which looks sort of like a golf club with a Frisbee attached to the bottom, uses magnetism to help people find hidden metal objects in the ground. The device uses an electric coil, producing a magnetic field. Most treasure hunters only find bottle caps, but you never know....

If you're riding in a car and stop at a red light, there may be an electrified wire loop stuck into the road's surface. Using a magnet, this loop detects metal when a car drives over it, and it sends a signal to the light to turn green.

Magnetism lets a vending machine figure out which coins you've inserted into it. It uses the magnetic field created by an electric current in metal coins to analyze the coins, figuring out how much metal each coin contains and, from that, figuring out which coin it is.

Strange but true!

Melting candy invented the microwave oven? You bet! A researcher working on electromagnetic energy for the Raytheon Company was walking near a magnetron (used in radar equipment) and noticed that the magnetron's microwaves reached through his clothing and melted a candy bar inside his pocket. He then tried cooking popcorn near the magnetron and later a raw egg. His discovery led his company to develop the first microwave ovens in 1946. (Popcorn has since become one of the most popular microwaveable foods— pretty cool, considering its place in microwave history.)

This is also how the walk-through metal detectors at airports work, for airline security screenings. (You go through a metal detector, while your luggage gets an X-ray.) A piece of metal—like some coins in your pocket—can set off the alarm in the metal detector. The screening agent will then use a handheld metal detector to find the cause.

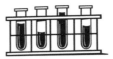

SENSING THE EARTH'S MAGNETIC FIELD

The Earth itself, which is mainly made of molten iron slosh-ing in liquid form at the center, is a giant magnet creating a strong magnetic field. Compasses work by sensing that magnetic field. The Earth's magnetic field also repels hazard-ous electromagnetic radiation from the sun. We would all get fried by the sun if too much of its radiation reached us.

Before satellites and GPS (global positioning systems), that field was a handy way for us to find our way around. It's still there. Find out for yourself by making your own compass.

To sense the Earth's magnetic field, you'll need a magnet, but not just any old magnet. The magnets you have on your refrigerator are not free to move, so they can't orient them-selves with the Earth's magnetic field.

Materials

- Bowl
- Thick magnet
- Needle or pins
- Styrofoam or cork
- Paper clips or pins
- Compass (optional)

Procedure

1. Fill a bowl of water for your magnet to float in. The bowl needs to be wide enough for the needle or pin to rotate without touching the sides. It does not need to be very deep. Make sure there are no magnets or electrical devices nearby.

2. Next, you need to magnetize a needle or pin. Most are made of steel, and steel can be magnetized with a real magnet. You need a thick magnet for this—most flat magnets have only a very thin layer of magnetic material, not enough to magnetize your needle. You can check the strength of your magnet by seeing whether it can pick up a few paper clips.

Magnetize your needle by stroking it across the magnet 10–40 times The stronger the magnet, the fewer strokes you need. When your needle is magnetized, it will stick to a paper clip and pick up pins. Do not keep your magnet near your bowl. Move it into another room.

continued ➡

3. Make your needle float by poking it through a very small piece of styrofoam—a pea-size piece of styrofoam is large enough. You could also use a piece of cork.

4. Rest your floating needle in the water and watch it until it stops rotating. It will take a few seconds. The needle will be oriented north/south. Make sure the needle is really oriented to the Earth's magnetic field by turning the bowl around. The needle will always point in the same direction, no matter how far you rotate the bowl.

5. If you want to know which end of the needle is pointing north and you don't know where north is, you can figure it out. Find the direction that the sun sets—that's west. Stretch out your left arm to the side and point west. You'll be facing north. Magnetic north is not always exactly the same as geographical north, but they're usually pretty close. You can also check the accuracy of your homemade compass by comparing it with a real compass if you have one.

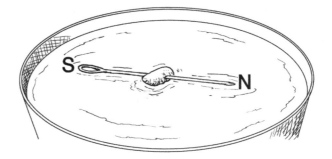

More things to investigate

How strong is the Earth's magnetic field? Move your magnet close to your homemade compass. If the magnet is near the bowl, does the needle change direction? Does that mean that your magnet is stronger than the Earth's magnetic field? How close do you have to move the magnet to affect the needle?

Take your bowl around the house, carrying it carefully to avoid spilling. Does electricity affect your homemade compass? Try your compass in different places to see whether the Earth's magnetic field is constant. If your compass is near an electrical appliance or a power strip, do you notice any changes?

How do you de-magnetize your compass? Will dropping it several times work? Can you heat it to de-magnetize it? What if you freeze it? Will it just de-magnetize over time if you ignore it?

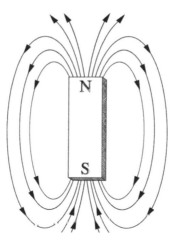

Which thing is actually alive? Your computer or that wiggly one-celled amoeba you studied in science class? Well, that's simple. For sure, it's got to be the amoeba. After all, a computer's not a living thing—it's a machine.

It's no surprise, though, if you have to think twice about whether your computer is, in fact, alive or not. Here's why: It shares certain qualities with living things. It can be infected by viruses, for example. It sometimes reacts in unpredictable ways. It is "nourished" by electricity.

Clearly, though, these qualities don't make your computer any more alive than a vacuum cleaner—although, BTW, some vacuums can clean perfectly well without any human help whatsoever. Still, even really smart vacuums that seem to move intelligently around your living-room floor are not alive.

What is true is that the line between man-made technology and life is getting thinner every day, because science keeps making gigantic leaps when it comes to creating artificial life.

Think about it. Not so very long ago, concepts like genetic engineering, cloning, nanotechnology, and DNA sequencing existed only in the minds of science-fiction writers. Now they're reality. Another example: Robots are reality today, too—and they're becoming more and more lifelike and more and more useful.

Bottom line, all these developments mean that even scientists have a little trouble explaining what "life" actually is.

WHAT IT TAKES TO BE "ALIVE"

You may have heard plenty about the "facts of life," but you've heard practically zilch about the facts scientists use to figure out what qualities make something alive. Here's one way of looking at what it takes to define a living being:

- A living thing is made out of cells.

- A living thing can't stay alive when its parts are separated and unconnected to each other (except for some slime molds, but that's another story....)

- A living thing takes in nourishment and chemically transforms it to provide energy.

- A living thing is able to adapt to its changing environment.

- A living thing can reproduce itself.

- A living thing eventually dies.

Even if you're not a scientist, you can poke holes in some of these statements. You can cut the arms and legs off most mammals, and the right doctors can make sure that they'll still survive. Worms will survive even if you cut them in half. On the other hand, if you disconnect the organs—like the heart, the liver, and especially the brain—of mammals or even simpler creatures, like worms, they'll die.

And there's more. Plenty of living things can't reproduce. For example, before maturity or past a certain age, most animals are unable to have babies. Another exception: mules. They can't reproduce, because they're born sterile. But if a mule ever kicks you, you'll know just how alive it is. Finally, at some life stages, like infancy and old age, many creatures need help adapting to their environments in order to survive. But surely, that doesn't mean our youngest and oldest aren't very much alive.

In general, though, these statements are simply guidelines, and like most of nature's rules and guidelines, there are always exceptions. Think of these guidelines as helpful statements that define what "life" actually means.

So now that you know, more or less, how to define life, you'll also want to know this: How did life begin?

THE BIRTH OF LIFE

Let's start with how old our planet is. To do the math, scientists began with the knowledge that our solar system is about 4.5 billion years old. Then they examined rocks and fossils found all over the world. By measuring the decay of radioactive isotopes (these remain radioactive practically forever) that occur naturally in rocks and minerals, they've concluded that the oldest rocks found, so far, are something like 4 billion years old and come from northwestern Canada.

The question that still boggles everyone's mind, scientists and school kids alike, is this: Just how, exactly, did life spring up from rock? Turns out, some scientists just might have an answer to that question. In 2011 scientists from Oxford University in England and the University of Western Australia teamed up on an interesting project that focused on pumice.

Pumice is a kind of light, frothy, porous volcanic rock. In fact, you may even have a piece hanging around in your bathroom, because its rough surface makes it the perfect thing for scrubbing off dead skin and calluses from your feet while you're bathing. You can buy a small hunk at any drugstore.

Life on the beach

The scientists discovered that pumice, besides being a handy personal grooming tool, also makes the perfect habitat for the earliest organisms that sprang into life around 3.4 billion years ago.

Pumice floats like a raft on water, and it can absorb metals and other substances, like phosphates. Scientists believe that all this stuff was in the recipe that helped create the Earth's earliest living microorganisms. As pumice bobbed along on the water of our baby planet, it was likely struck by volcanic lightning, soaked by chemicals those volcanoes produced, and radiated by the sun.

The research team said that these dramatic conditions might have triggered the chemical chain reaction that created the first living cells. Life, they say, may have begun thriving in damp, sandy places—think beaches—composed largely of pumice. This is just one theory out there. Other scientists think life may have started in clay, or around deep-sea volcanic vents, or even in outer space. Nobody knows the origins of life for certain...yet.

From nothing to something

Eventually, out of this rich, murky, chemical stew, life emerged. Naturally, it was pretty simple. At first, living beings took shape as one-celled bacteria called **archae** (from the Greek word for "old"). Though no fossils exist, scientists say that these microscopic creatures are likely as old as the Earth itself.

At first, the tiny bacteria were **anaerobic,** meaning that oxygen was poisonous to them, so they subsisted on whatever other gases the Earth produced at that time. A good thing, too, evolution-wise, because back then there wasn't a lot of oxygen on our planet.

Eventually, another form of bacteria, **cyanobacteria**, developed, and this is where life forms began to get really interesting. That's because cyanobacteria used water to produce oxygen. Pretty soon these one-celled bacteria formed huge colonies in shallow seawater. The oxygen these colonies produced, along with the other gases that archea and other bacteria produced, became the basis for a more stable atmosphere on our planet. Once the atmosphere was more stable, the Earth became more comfortable for new living things. Eventually, the colonies of bacteria produced enough oxygen to allow for the development of new life forms that depended on oxygen. Like us. Eventually.

🔬 Discover this!

Starfish eat clams. Wondering how? In what may be one of the coolest of all the animal adaptations, a starfish will actually wrap its arms (they have five) around the clam and pull its shell apart. Then it inserts its stomach into the opened shell and releases enzymes that partially digest the creature. Next, the starfish sucks what's left of the clam into its body to finish off the process of digesting it.

THE GREAT DARWIN

In the 1830s the English botanist Charles Darwin shipped out from England to tag along with a mapping expedition of the Pacific and South America. Darwin was just 22 years old, and when the boat docked at the Galapagos Islands off the coast of Ecuador, his life took an exciting turn. The animals he saw in the Galapagos inspired Darwin to develop ideas that changed the way we understand life—today we know it as the **theory of evolution.** Darwin was struck by how very different the creatures he saw on these islands were, compared to those he knew back in England.

Being a young man with keen powers of observation, he noticed something that other people might have missed. All of the 12 major islands in the chain had the same species of little birds called finches. But, depending on which island the birds lived on, the shapes of their beaks were different—in some cases, by a quite a lot. When he looked more closely at their eating habits and the foods available on each island, Darwin realized that the differently shaped beaks allowed the finches to dine on whatever was available on their home island.

Today we count 13 different species of these birds, now known as Darwin's Finches, on the Galapagos Islands. The cactus-eaters, for example, have long, sharp bills that let them dig through thick cactus skin to get to the sweet, juicy flesh. Ground finches have beaks that let them crush the ticks they pick off iguanas and land tortoises. And the vampire finch has. What else? A needle-sharp beak that lets the finches suck blood from poor masked and red-footed boobies (another bird).

So, Darwin figured, the finches had totally adapted to their surroundings. But how? Darwin's answer was that somehow the creatures were able to thrive by shape-shifting their beaks, over time and over generations, so that they could be efficient eaters of the food in their habitats.

Darwin dubbed the process "natural selection" and came up with the theory of evolution.

Like Newton's discovery of gravity, Darwin's theory of evolution brought understanding to many huge scientific questions. He helped explain the environment—and how its specific demands helped shape the living things that inhabited it. Only the creatures best adapted to their environments could survive, he said, and the concept of "survival of the fittest" was born.

Why every living thing has two names

You can thank Carolus Linnaeus for the fact that all living things have two names. In 1735 this Swedish medical doctor published a little pamphlet called *Systema Naturae*, or *System of Nature*. It described his original system of classifying all living things, which sorted life into groups based on their shared similarities. It was his idea to create a two-name ("binomial") system for naming every living creature—we still use his system today. It calls for a Latin name for the genus (a grouping of living things that share common characteristics), and another name for the species (a grouping of living things that can interbreed with each other). So that's why human beings are also known as **Homo sapiens.**

SIX FORMS OF LIFE

Although it's way beyond the realm of possibility to take a census of *every* living thing on the planet, it is certainly possible to take a look at the kinds of living things we know we share with planet Earth.

When Linnaeus first created his naming system, he created just two classifications, or "kingdoms"—plants and animals. But over the years, the development of powerful microscopes allowed scientists to discover whole new worlds of life. Some scientists count six kingdoms into which we can classify all the living things on our planet: plants, animals, protists, fungi, archaebacteria, and eubacteria—but our classification systems are constantly changing.

Let's take a look at each kingdom.

Animal. There are over 1 million known animal species alive today. Many animals are **heterotrophs;** they must eat various kinds of foods to survive (you might also hear them called **omnivores**).

Fact: Animal kingdom members live in every different kind of environment on Earth.

Plants. The kingdom of plants contains over 250,000 species, and its members range from tiny moss plants to giant redwood trees, which can top 300 feet (91 m) tall. Plants are "autotrophs," meaning they are organisms that make their own food.

Fact: Without plants, life as we know it would not exist. Plants feed almost every other living thing on the planet.

Archaebacteria. These one-celled creatures are Earth's oldest form of life.

Fact: Archaebacteria live in extreme environments. Some are adapted to temperatures hot enough to boil water—in fact, in 1983 scientists were shocked to discover archaebacteria living deep under the Pacific Ocean in a pool of hot gases and molten rock. Others can live in the arctic ice.

Eubacteria. These are the most common bacteria on Earth and, like archaebacteria, are one-celled and live in colonies.

Fact: Some eubacteria cause disease, including streptococci, which cause painful strep throat. But others are helpful, including those that live in your digestive system.

Fungi. Yeasts, molds, and mushrooms are all members of the fungi kingdom. About 75,000 species have been identified, but scientists believe as many as a million more are waiting to be discovered. Fungi are also heterotrophs.

Fact: Some fungi, including mushrooms and truffles, are delicious, but others are poisonous. Never, ever eat mushrooms you find in the wild, even if they look identical to the kind you buy in the store.

Protists. This class is kind of a catch-all group, because it includes all microorganisms that aren't bacteria, fungi, plants, or animals. Examples of protists are slime molds and algae.

Fact: Most protists have only one cell and are larger than bacteria. In addition, their cells are more complex than bacteria.

More alike than different?

We humans think we've cornered the market on the higher powers of thinking. We may even believe that we're the extreme top of the food chain, that we're smarter and more sophisticated than all the other animals. But maybe we should think again. These examples of animal behavior are pretty awesome—and very human.

Using tools
Ravens use stones to crack eggs. Sometimes they even brace the egg on one stone and use another to get the job done.

Sense of humor
There's a famous film of a gibbon (a type of ape) that's clearly enjoying teasing two tiger cubs. He pulls their ears and tails, leaps up into the trees to escape their claws, and pounces again once their backs are turned.

Memory

Certain birds can remember where they've stashed seeds for at least six months—and can keep track of up to 5,000 locations in a 15-mile (24-km) area.

Math skills

Chimpanzees can do simple addition.

Awareness of self

It's said that great apes, dolphins, elephants, and magpies can recognize themselves in a mirror.

Empathy

Elephants feed and wait for disabled herd mates.

ANIMAL ODDITIES—
NOT SO ODD, AFTER ALL

You may wonder why crickets have their ears on their legs, shrimp have their hearts in their heads, or why starfish can turn their stomachs inside out—ugh!—but the answers would have made a lot of sense to Charles Darwin. These "oddities," as it turns out, are actually special adaptations these animals have made over time that allow them to survive and thrive in their particular habitat. Let's take a closer look at some of these animal oddities.

Crickets have musical wings—and ears on their knees

Sound and crickets go hand in hand. Their loud chirping enlivens evenings in summer and especially during the fall. Ever wonder why these shiny black insects make so much noise?

The answer is survival. Crickets need to mate and lay as many eggs as they can, because all adult crickets die as soon as winter arrives. So the males get busy trying to call the right girl, chirping away by drawing their wings together. One wing has a sharp edge that it scrapes over its other wing, which is ridged like a file. Since not all crickets are built exactly alike, each male produces sound that's a little different from his buddies. In fact, the males send out different tones—some to attract females and others to warn off other males.

Females listen for that chirping and seek out the best musicians as mates. It's all about survival—the strongest male chirpers are likely to have stronger cricket sons and daughters.

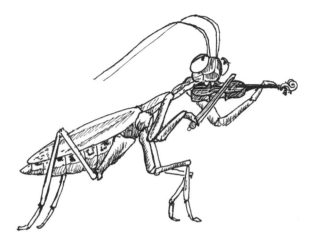

Hearing all these different kinds of chirping is dependent on having a great set of ears. And crickets' ears are so terrific that they're the insect version of Surround Sound! Their ears are located on the cricket's front pair of legs, right at their knees. The ears receive sound in four different ears, and by facing one way or the other, a cricket can tell which direction sound is coming from. This adaptation helps males and females find each other during mating season—and that helps the cricket species survive.

🔬 **Discover this!**

Crickets chirp in "time" to the temperature—if you count the number of chirps you hear in 15 seconds and add 37, you'll come close to knowing how hot it is—or isn't—outside.

Bet you didn't know...

Q. ...where shrimps' hearts are located.

A. In their heads! The part of the shrimp we eat is actually the abdomen, which is a strong muscle that helps it swim. A shrimp's "head," located in a body section called the "carapace," is protected by a thicker shell than the rest of its body. The heart, brain, and other vital organs are all located within the carapace.

Q. ...what animal lays the largest eggs of any on the planet.

A. That would be the ostrich. Its eggs measure about 6 by 5 inches (15 x 13 cm), and can weigh a whopping three pounds. Some say that whale sharks' eggs are the largest in the animal kingdom, because an egg recovered from a whale shark measured 12 by 5.5 inches (30 x 14 cm). But that was based on just one discarded egg discovered in 1955. Figuring out an average size for a shark's egg is a pretty tricky business, because female whale sharks keep their fertilized eggs inside their bodies, then bear live young.

Q. ...sharks could help with cancer research.

A. The cancer rate of sharks is much lower than ours, which has led some experts to believe that sharks are cancer-free creatures. So, they thought, if sharks don't get cancer, maybe something in their bodies could protect humans from developing the disease. Scientists honed in on shark cartilage, because experiments seemed to show that it contained chemical compounds that could shut down the formation of blood vessels that cancer tumors need in order to grow. As a result, companies sprang up to sell shark cartilage products to protect against cancer, and these products became extremely popular.

EXPERIMENT

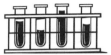

WHERE WILL YEAST BE THE FITTEST?

If three colonies of baker's yeast hitched a ride and landed on an island where there were no humans baking bread, could they survive and reproduce? If it rained on the island, the yeast would eventually be washed into the ocean or into a freshwater pool. The pool might be clean spring water or the pool might have other substances in it. You can test which environment might favor the survival of the yeast colony using freshwater, saltwater like the ocean, and sugar water.

When yeast grows, it gives off carbon dioxide, just like you do when you breathe out. In bread we can see the holes where the gas came out. In water you will see foam containing carbon dioxide bubbles when the yeast is growing.

Can you find out which water environment favors growth and survival of a yeast colony?

continued ▶

Materials

- Baker's yeast (you can buy packets of active dry yeast)
- Water
- Sugar
- Salt
- Optional (but lots of fun): fruit juice, soda pop, vinegar, milk, honey, flour… Be creative.
- Clear, tall drinking glasses or narrow, tall, clear glass jars
- Measuring teaspoon
- ¼ cup measure
- Spoon or chopstick for mixing

Procedure

1. Set up your water environments: Label each container so you know what will be in each one.

2. Add ¼ cup of warm water to three glasses.

3. Add 1 teaspoon of salt to one glass and 1 teaspoon of sugar to the other glass. Mix those glasses with a spoon or a chopstick. Leave one glass with just water (to represent a freshwater pond) as your control.

4. Add 1 teaspoon of yeast to each container.

5. Check on your yeast in about half an hour and again at one hour. If the yeast colonies are growing, you should see that the mixture has foam on top and it smells "yeasty." The higher the foam is, the more the yeast is growing. It should be easy to determine if fresh-, saltwater, or sugar water is more favorable for survival of the yeast.

More things to investigate

Do you think you could make the yeast grow faster? Could the foam get higher? If you add more things, will it grow better? Is there anything that stops it from growing? Perhaps there are other combinations you would like to test out. Choose one or more of the optional ingredients to see if any of them make yeast grow. You can also try changing the water temperatures: Is it better hotter or colder?

WHAT WE ARE AND HOW WE WORK

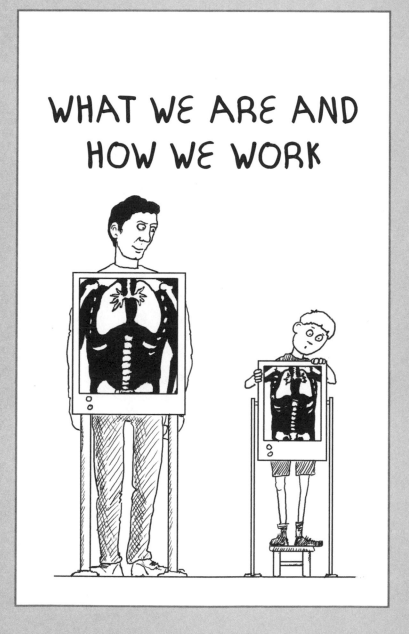

Humans—we're a pretty amazing species, don't you think? We may not be as fast as a cheetah or as strong as an ox (Q. Just how strong is an ox, anyway? A. Strong enough to pull two cars all by itself!) We also can't fly like a falcon, swim like a dolphin, or race up a tree like a squirrel.

But we have plenty in common with all of those animals. Like other animals, we have a standard-issue bunch of organs that work pretty much the same way in us as they do in other creatures.

We have lungs for processing oxygen, a heart for pumping it through blood vessels to all parts of the body, a stomach and intestines (large and small) for digesting food, and a liver and a pair of kidneys for filtering out waste.

Eyes for seeing, ears for hearing, skin for feeling and protecting. All help keep us alert, aware—and alive.

THE BRAIN: NATURE'S GIFT TO HUMANS

And, like most animals, we also have a brain. Although the human brain isn't the largest one in the animal kingdom, even in relation to our body size, its inner wiring is complex to the point of mind-boggling. Weighing in at about three pounds, our brains contain some 100 billion nerve cells, called neurons, each of which has between 1,000 and 10,000 synapses that branch off to send the cell's messages on to other cells. Think of these synapses as the "highways" along which nerve signals flow. These signals send messages throughout your body signal everything from your regular heartbeat and breathing (even while you're asleep) to helping you write a sentence, kick a soccer ball, or paint a picture.

When it comes to memory storage, your brain is pretty remarkable. Because of the way the neurons connect with each other, you can store something like a million gigabytes of memory, which equals one petabyte. How big is that? Well, according to a report on one technology website, the 3D movie *Avatar* takes up one petabyte of storage, which is roughly equal to a 32-year-long MP3 file! (So when it comes to forgetting your homework, sorry—no excuses!)

You're a brainiac

Your brain sets off alarms whenever you feel even a twinge of pain, but it can feel no pain itself. It's mostly water—80 percent H_2O, to be exact—and takes up just 2 percent of your body's weight. Although it has no muscles and doesn't move, your brain is an energy hog that gobbles up 20 percent of the oxygen you take in and uses a full 25 percent of your body's energy supply.

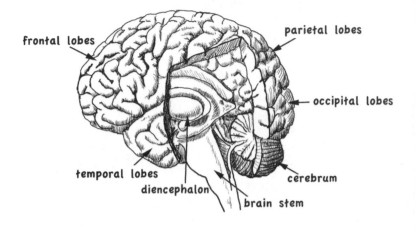

frontal lobes

parietal lobes

occipital lobes

temporal lobes

diencephalon

cerebrum

brain stem

Whales, dolphins, and elephants may have bigger brains than we do, but a key part of the human brain, called the **cerebrum**, is far more advanced than in those very intelligent animals. It accounts for about 85 percent of the entire brain's weight.

The four lobes of the cerebrum are what help make us human. The **frontal lobes**, right behind your forehead, are responsible for speech, thought, learning, emotion, and movement. Next to them, the **parietal lobes** help you process input from your senses of touch and also monitor temperature and pain. The **occipital lobes** deal with vision, while the **temporal lobes** are concerned with hearing and memory.

In a nutshell, our brain's cerebrum is largely responsible for what makes us who we are.

Besides the **cerebrum**, other parts of the brain include the cerebellum, which is responsible for organizing muscle movement and maintaining your balance.

A lemon-size brain structure, called the **diencephalon**, includes two major, but tiny, parts: the thalamus and the hypothalamus. The thalamus receives nerve impulses from all over the body and relays them to the correct area of the brain for processing. The hypothalamus regulates hormones (chemical messengers in your body) made by its neighbor, the pituitary gland. These chemical messengers regulate your growth and other key life-sustaining behaviors, including eating, drinking, and even reproduction.

Finally, at the base of your brain is the **brain stem**, which takes care of the automatic functions that keep you alive. It controls your breathing, heart rate, and blood pressure. What's more, it tells you when you're feeling alert and when you're feeling sleepy.

Talking—and art—make us unique

We are certainly not the only beings on the planet who communicate with each other. From ants to octopi to dolphins to baboons, most animals rely on more or less complicated forms of communication. But humans are the only beings who communicate by using language. And that's not all that sets us apart from other mammals. We are also unique in our drive, ability, and talent for using art, theater, dance, and music to express ourselves emotionally.

If you're thinking to yourself that birds, crickets, and frogs also seem to express themselves musically, for example, that's a good point. But there's a big difference between human music and animal music. So far as we know, most sounds that animals make are genetically programmed and are mostly mating calls or warnings to other animals either to stay away or that there's danger around. Human music can express so many more emotions and meanings than that.

OUR NUTS AND BOLTS—
OUR BONES

Of the million or more species in the animal kingdom, we are in the tiny 2 percent of animals who have bones. That makes us vertebrates. The rest of the animals on the planet are invertebrates. Instead of bones, they may have shells, like clams; hard outer coverings, like insects; or fluid-filled "skin," like jellyfish and worms. It's our framework of bones—our skeleton—that gives us our shape and helps hold us together when we move.

Your bones grow and change throughout your life. For example, newborn babies come into this world with more bones in their bodies than adults—300, to be exact. And some of those aren't even bone—they're a softer, more flexible material called cartilage. As you grow, the cartilage hardens into

Smelly feet?

Our feet are covered in 250,000 sweat glands that can produce as much as a cup of sweat a day. And if you blame that, um, aromatic odor on the sweat itself, think again: Foot stench actually comes from millions of bacteria that multiply on your sweat-soaked socks and shoes. And PS: It's not the microscopic bacteria that smell—it's their, um, waste products. Ick!

bone, and some of those 300 bones fuse together to eventually form the 206 bones that make up every adult skeleton. This happens by the time you are age 25 or so.

Some of our bone networks are amazingly complex and perfectly suited to the special needs of human existence. Your spine, for example, helps hold the body upright and protects the spinal column. Your ribs form the flexible "armor" that protect your internal organs. Your skull, which is made up of several bones, not just one, protects your brain and gives your face its unique shape.

And then there's your feet and legs.

Strong and healthy

Since the mineral calcium is critical for healthy bone development, it's important that young people eat a varied diet that contains some low-fat dairy products and dark, leafy green vegetables, which are calcium-rich.

🔬 Discover this!

The largest and strongest bone in your body is one of your leg bones. Called the femur, it's the bone that runs from your pelvis to your knee. That's why it's also sometimes called the thigh bone.

Our feet give us the ability to stand and walk, and they're amazingly complicated. Each foot contains 26 bones each, one quarter of all the bones in our bodies. They're specially designed to be flat and wide, which helps you balance when you're walking—and they're designed to absorb the tons of impact they bear from just walking around every day. On a very active day, feet carry the average person about 9,000 steps, which over a lifetime adds up to five or six strolls around the world.

When it comes to survival, the ability to run—not only to get away from threats but also to catch up with prey—was a major adaptation for humans (and many other species, too). The bones in your legs are especially big and strong—they need to be, to support the weight of your body, especially when it's moving.

EYE ON YOUR EYES

The eyes of chameleons, scorpions, or dragonflies are pretty amazing. An old world chameleon can swivel its eyes around independently, so that the creature can actually see in two directions at once. Scorpions have as many as 12 eyes (the better to sting you with?), and the eyes of the dragonfly can contain 30,000 lenses. Tropical fish and other brightly colored animals have more color vision cells than we do, meaning they can see colors when we cannot.

Still, our basic human eyes are nearly miraculous structures that give humans one of their most important senses—sight.

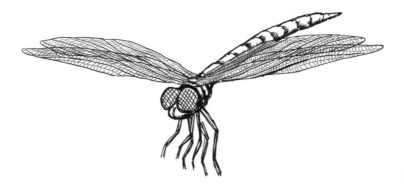

Our eyes are in nearly constant motion, and this not only helps us see, it also helps keeps our eyes healthy. In fact, your eyes continually make tiny movements. These little eyeball twitches help your eye take in new information, and that allows you to see images.

Healthy eyes

To keep your eyes healthy, it's a good idea to train yourself to blink regularly, especially when you're reading, using a computer, or watching TV or a movie.

Blink and you'll miss it?

The other essential movement your eyes make is blinking. Think of it as a built-in eyeball self-cleaning device. You blink, depending on the conditions, something like once every five seconds, for a whopping 17,000 times a day—or 6.25 million times a year! Pretty impressive. Each time you blink, your eye shuts for 0.3 seconds, which gives you 30 minutes of shut-eye (not counting sleep time) each day.

Blinking regularly and frequently is essential for the health of your eyes. Every time you blink, three different layers of tears coat your eyes. The first is rich in protein and provides a base for the second layer to stick to. That second layer of tears helps wash away dust, pollen, and other debris. It's also like a vitamin for your eyes, because the middle layer of tears is laced with minerals your eyes need, plus moisture and protein.

Finally, the third layer of tears is slightly oily and keeps the middle layer of lubrication in place longer. It lubricates the surface of your eyes and the inside of your eyelids.

Baby, what big eyes you have—and Grandpa, what a big nose and ears you have!

It's a fact of life that, in proportion to their other body parts, babies' eyes are actually quite large. In fact, at birth a baby's eyes measure about 18 m around, which is about 75 percent the size of an adult's eye. The eyes will grow very slowly until they reach their adult size of about 25 m—about 1 inch. At about that time, the bony eye socket that holds the eyeball also stops growing.

Unlike your eyes, which stop growing while you're still in college, two other body parts keep growing…and growing…and growing. That would be your nose and ears, which explains why these two body parts may seem extra large on older people.

How come? Ears and noses are made of cartilage, which unlike bone, continues to grow until the day you die. What's more, earlobes stretch as we age, which makes ears look even larger than they are.

THE SKINNY ON SKIN

The largest organ in the human body is the one that's outside our bodies—our skin. An average adult has about eight pounds of it, which if you stretched it out, would cover about 22 square feet (7 m).

Space: the anti-aging miracle?

You may have read that when astronauts travel through outer space, they don't get any older. That notion comes from a theory, known as Einstein's Twin Paradox, by the great physicist Albert Einstein. The theory asks you to imagine identical twin brothers. One is an astronaut who takes off into outer space. The other remains behind on Earth. When the astronaut twin returns home, the brothers are amazed to discover that the astronaut twin is younger than his stay-at-home brother.

Huh? Another classic Einstein theory, called the theory of relativity, states that the faster you travel through space, the slower you travel through time. If that were true, it would mean that rocketing to a galaxy far, far away could be the secret to staying forever young. Except it probably isn't true.

Scientists working on that theory today believe that, in fact, traveling through space will have the opposite effect on humans, because the theory doesn't take into account the fact that space travelers would be exposed to untold amounts of radiation. The radiation can damage an astronaut's DNA—and that can cause aging.

All of this is still unknown. We won't know for sure what effects space travel has on the aging process until NASA sends astronauts outside of Earth's orbit. So far, astronauts have only traveled inside Earth's orbit, where they're protected from harmful cosmic rays by Earth's protective magnetic shield. Plans are said to be on the drawing board for a trip to Mars in 2018, at which point we might learn more about the effects of space travel on the aging process.

WE HAVE FINGERNAILS—
AND TOENAILS—NOT CLAWS

Even biologists (scientists who specialize in living things) are a little stumped when it comes to explaining why we have fingernails and toenails. They may have evolved from claws of ancient reptiles, but biologists aren't certain about this. What we know for sure is that most primates (the group of mammals that includes humans, apes, lemurs, marmosets, and monkeys) have fingernails. We also know that nails are made from keratin, a biological material that makes up a wide variety of things that cover animal skin—including claws, feathers, scales, horns, and hair.

Fingernails are handy for humans to have, because they help us perform certain tasks, like peeling oranges, for example. And they probably help protect our delicate fingers and toes from injury. We have more nerve endings in our fingers and toes than we do in most other parts of our body, which is one reason why it's so important to keep them safe.

Our fingernails grow more than twice as fast as toenails (scientists at the University of North Carolina actually studied this). Your pinky grows slower than your other nails, and you big toenail grows faster than its neighbors. Nails usually grow faster in the summer than the winter, and nails on your dominant hand tend to grow faster than on your other hand. It usually takes about three to six months for a new fingernail to grow out completely, but it'll take between a year and 18 months for a toenail to grow out completely.

CAUTION: READING THIS WILL MAKE YOUR SKIN CRAWL

Oooh, you've got cooties! No, really, you do—we all do. In fact, the human body is (literally) crawling with bacteria. There may be more than 100 different varieties of bacteria that dwell in communities on our skin.

A huge scientific program, called the Human Micro-Biome Project, was created at the National Institutes of Health to learn more about these non-human parts of us and to learn about the effects these bacteria have on health and disease.

The scientists collected bacteria from 20 places on the bodies of 10 healthy people who had volunteered to be part of the project. They took samples from all kinds of skin—from between the toes, inside the belly button, and even right between the eyes.

From the perspective of bacteria, the human body is a little like the planet Earth: A place with many different habitats that house many different species of bacteria. Some bacteria prefer the drier, more "desertlike" areas of the skin, like the inside of your arm or on your back. Others thrive in moister, wetter "jungle" areas, like your underarms or inside your nose, for example.

Although we usually think of bacteria as germs that cause illness, researchers think that some bacteria may actually help keep us from getting sick.

In the future the scientists working on this project will be comparing bacteria living on the skin of healthy people with bacteria on the skin of people who are sick. This, they hope, will help them make connections between skin-dwelling bacteria and certain illnesses, including skin diseases like eczema, for example.

HEALING—A PRETTY AMAZING PROCESS

Scraping your knee, cutting your finger, breaking your arm—these are painful but common accidents that happen to young people (and older people, too) no matter how careful they try to be. It's just a fact of life that active kids will eventually get banged up a little. A Band-Aid and antiseptic take care of most boo-boos, while more serious injuries may require a trip to the doctor or even to the ER. Given proper care and some time, these wounds will heal.

But how?

Healing is a process that involves four rather complicated steps.

Say you cut yourself. The cut begins to bleed, but almost right away your body takes action to stop the bleeding. First, blood vessels in the area narrow, and that slows or stops the flow of blood. Then, your body releases a substance called adenosine diphosphate (ADP), which helps your blood clot and create a blockage that stops the bleeding.

During the second step, your body sends out substances that attempt to kill germs that might cause infection (you can help this process along by gently washing the wound with mild soap and water and applying an antiseptic). Your body's infection-fighting substances, called **cytokines,** create inflammation, which reddens the area around a wound. The redness is a signal that the body's healing response is occurring.

Next, the body works on repairing or replacing damaged tissue. Any broken blood vessels are rebuilt, and the body creates new tissue to fill in the wounded area. This process, called **regeneration,** takes several days to complete. In the final step, called **remodeling,** the body strengthens the new tissue until the wound is healed completely.

WHO HAS GREATER LUNG CAPACITY: YOU OR YOUR PARENTS?

Lungs are made of a spongelike material. This construction means most of the organ is not tissue, but air. Lung capacity is a measurement of how much air your lungs can hold. The more air you can hold, the faster your body can move oxygen to your muscles to make them work better.

Materials

- Small bucket or large bowl
- 2-quart plastic bottle
- Straws or clean tubing
- Measuring cup or graduated cylinder
- Marker or masking tape
- Clear packing tape for taping straws together (optional)

Procedure

1. Fill a bucket about half full and fill the 2-quart plastic bottle most of the way full.

2. Quickly tip your bottle upside down, with your fingers over the opening, and lower the bottle into the bucket, keeping it upside down and your fingers over the opening.

3. Remove your finger quickly so that the bottle remains mostly full of water. A second person can help you keep the bottle balanced upside down in the bucket, because it can be hard to hold it. Most of the water should still remain in the bottle.

4. Bend a straw and carefully insert it into the upside-down bottle, keeping the end free for you to blow into. You may wish to use two straws taped together to give you a longer tube.

5. Mark the water level in your bottle with a marker.

6. Now breathe OUT normally into the straw until you have no more air. Watch the level of water in the bottle drop, and mark the level when you have no more air.

7. Take the bottle out. Fill up your bottle to the first mark. Then measure how much water it takes to fill it up to the second mark with measuring cups or a graduated cylinder. The amount of water you used is your lung capacity.

8. Compare your lung capacity with others'. Remember, if you want to draw a scientific conclusion, you will have to measure a lot of people to get a good sample.

WHY EARTH LOOKS (AND ACTS) LIKE EARTH

When we talk about the early days of the Earth, we're talking about a very different planet than the one we know. Today we think of a landscape made up of very different features—oceans, lakes, and seas surrounding continents and islands marked by mountains and hills, prairies and deserts. But it took around 500 million years of cooling before these features even started to form.

THE COOL PLANET

BOOM! Somewhere in outer space a star explodes. Enormous amounts of fiery hot gas and dust go flying from the site of the explosion.

CRASH! That's how our solar system began—with an enormous explosion and a collision of space stuff. Some of the stuff flying off from the explosion of the star crashed into a gas cloud, and with a huge impact. Fiery hot gases and dust particles and space junk came together, forming lumps. The lumps began to clump together, getting bigger and bigger. Eventually one of the clumps toward the middle of the mess, the biggest and heaviest and hottest one, became awesomely hot. That clump is our sun.

All the other stuff started rotating around the sun. As everything slowly, slowly cooled off (seriously slowly; we're talking billions of years here), more lumps began to form, first the size of grains of rice, then more like pebbles, then like rocks, then like boulders... OK, you get the picture. Eventually, these lumps became big enough to become planets, and they eventually found a regular pattern of orbiting around the sun. One of these planets is the Earth. And today, billions of years later, it's still cooling off.

Cosmic crashes

Today we think of the solar system as a peaceful and orderly place (a few mad meteors flying around are the exception), but in the earliest days it was a pretty rough neighborhood. Space junk was forever colliding with planets. These collisions did some important things around 4.5 billion years ago.

- Mars used to be a lot closer to the Earth than it is today, until a crash pushed it farther away from the sun.

- Another crash whacked the Earth into its present position and tipped it at an angle, so its rotation gives us the seasons.

- Scientists believe that the moon was formed when one really huge piece of space rubble, probably as big as Mars, smashed into the Earth. This crash broke a piece of Earth's outer layer loose and sent it flying, but it didn't get far enough to escape Earth's gravitational pull. The piece that broke off—that's the moon.

- The moon also owes its appearance to space crashes. Scientists think all the craters are left over from impacts with meteors.

Layer upon layer

As the Earth cooled down, we ended up with a planet made up of lots of rock. And as it cooled, it separated into three main layers.

The **crust** is the outer layer of the planet. When you stand on the ground, you're standing on the very outermost layer of the crust. It's the thinnest of the Earth's layers—at the most, it's around 25 miles (40 km) thick, and at its thinnest, under the oceans, it's only around 5 miles (8 km) thick. The crust is mainly made up of two volcanic rocks, granite and basalt.

The **mantle** is the Earth's middle layer. It's around 1,800 miles (2,900 km) thick, and it's made up of **magma**, which is basically melted rocks. The rocks have melted in this layer because it's so hot there—around 3,600°F (2,000°C).

The core is at the center of the Earth. Scientists don't really know much about this layer, because it's so deep down that they've never been able to look at it or even test it. However, they're pretty sure that it's burning hot down there, with temperatures as high as 12,600°F (7,000°C).

Wait a minute. Didn't we just say that the Earth had cooled down? Well, it sure did. You can walk barefoot without getting burned, right? That's incredibly cooler than in the early days of our planet.

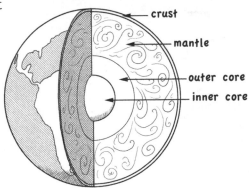

crust

mantle

outer core

inner core

Journey to the center of the Earth

From the Earth's surface to the center of the core is about 4,000 miles (6,400 km). You think that's a long way? Think again. It's only about the distance from Chicago, Illinois, to London, England, a trip people make every day. But the deepest hole ever drilled into the Earth, the Kola Superdeep Borehole in Russia, got down only a little more than 7.5 miles (12 km).

🔬 Discover this!

Earth is known as a terrestrial planet because it's made mainly of rock. Mercury, Venus, and Mars are also terrestrial planets. Some of the other planets in our solar system are called gas giants, because they're made mainly of gas. Jupiter, Saturn, Uranus, and Neptune are gas giants.

PLANETARY BURPS

At the same time as the Earth's rocky layers were forming, the rocky parts of the planet were separating out from the watery oceans and the gassy atmosphere. Scientists are not sure how things ended up layered this way. Some believe that the planet burped, spitting out the air and the water that was trapped in the rocks that were forming. (Scientists don't really call this burping. They call it outgassing. Yes, that's a pretty funny word, too.) Other scientists think that the water and air were brought to Earth by still more cosmic collisions. As gassy comets hit the Earth, they released some of their gases, creating the atmosphere and water.

Continents, mountains, volcanoes

Planetary burps don't completely explain why the landscape all around you looks the way it does. The Earth didn't burp out North America or Europe. The continents were formed as the Earth's crust shifted into place. And that shifting is still going on today.

The crust is made up of many separate pieces, called **plates,** that fit snugly together, meeting under oceans and seas. Some plates—ones that are completely under oceans and seas— are lower than others. Other plates carry the continents on their backs. All these plates are floating on top of the liquid mantle layer, and they are constantly moving, bringing the oceans and the continents with them. Most of the time, you don't notice the movement, and most of the movement is really, really slow.

Scientists who study the movement of these plates call what they do **plate tectonics.** Plate tectonics explains a lot of things, from how the continents were formed to why there are earthquakes and volcanic eruptions.

Minding the map

When you look at a globe or a world map, have you ever noticed that South America looks like it could neatly fit alongside Africa, like two pieces of a jigsaw puzzle? Back in 1912 a German geographer named Alfred Wegener noticed the same thing, and he came up with the idea that the continents are floating around and that they were once joined together in a supercontinent he named **Pangaea,** from the Greek words that mean "one earth." His theory came to be known the **continental drift theory.** The idea is that the continents are just drifting around on the surface of the Earth. Wegener himself was not really sure why the continents were slowly sailing around—he thought it might have had something to do with the Earth's daily rotation, creating kind of a sloshing effect. But because he couldn't prove his own idea, nobody took him seriously—at least, at the time.

Over the years, however, many scientists began to see that there was a lot of evidence for Wegener's idea of a supercontinent. For example, some geologists noticed that there are a lot of natural similarities between Africa and South America, especially in the rocks you find on both continents. They also pointed out that the fossils of a prehistoric reptile called the **mesosaurus,** which lived around 300 million years ago, are found both in South America and in Africa, but only in those two places. Since the mesosaurus couldn't swim that far and it couldn't fly, how did it manage to live on both continents?

Because of this kind of evidence, scientists agree that all the continents were once joined up in a huge single supercontinent. This is what the globe looked like 250 million years ago. All kinds of reptiles roamed **Pangaea,** and fish swam in the giant ocean surrounding the land. Around this time the earliest mammals and the earliest dinosaurs were starting to appear.

Around 200 million years ago Pangaea started to break apart. It first split into two, a giant northern continent called **Laurasia** and a giant southern one called **Gondwana**, which drifted apart. Dinosaurs and mammals floated on the two new continents.

Things were quiet for a little while (if 65 million years can be considered "a little while"). Then around 135 million years ago, Gondwana and Laurasia started breaking up. Gondwana split into two parts: Today we call them South America and Africa. India broke off from Africa and started floating north.

By around 40 million years ago the Earth started to take on a more familiar form. India crashed into Eurasia and became part of that continent. North America and Greenland floated

away from Europe, and Australia and Antarctica also drifted apart. It was too late for the dinosaurs—they were already extinct—but many mammals you would recognize today were already living on the new continents.

MOVING MOUNTAINS

You might not realize it, but the continents are still changing shape and moving around today. Since this kind of change takes such a very, very long time, we don't notice it...at least, not very often. But reminders of this process are all around us. Many of the majestic mountain ranges on the Earth were created by the movement of the plates.

The plates that make up the crust are constantly moving and changing. As old crust melts back into the mantle (the red-hot middle layer of our planet), new crust is created—this happens as magma (what the mantle is called when it moves up to the surface of the Earth) comes up from the mantle and solidifies. This process takes around 100 million years, and much of it happens under the ocean (no wonder we don't notice!). The new crust develops in a different place from where the old crust dissolves, so as each plate develops, it shifts a little bit. And as one plate moves, it pushes its neighbor, and that one pushes its neighbor, and so on and so on. Like we said, constant motion. Just very, very slow.

Many mountains are formed at places where two plates meet and collide. These mountains are known as **fold mountains,** and they usually have steep, pointy tops. The Himalayas are a dramatic reminder of a long-ago collision—somewhere around 40 million years ago, when India crashed into Eurasia. The smaller plate that India is riding on crashed into the much bigger plate that carries Eurasia with such force that the gigantic edges of each plate crumpled up. The result: some of the highest mountains on Earth, including Mount Everest, which challenge the world's best mountain climbers. But we're not talking about a car crash kind of collision. This is a very, very, very slow collision, taking millions of years. And in fact, this crumpling is still going on. Scientists estimate that the Himalayas are growing around 2 inches (5 cm) a year.

It's your fault!

Other mountains are formed along fault lines, places where two plates meet but don't collide. Sometimes as the two plates move past each other, they rub, leaving rough edges that sometimes get stacked on each other. An example of this type of "rough edge" mountain range is the Sierra Nevada Mountains in California.

Mountains can also form if magma from the mantle pushes its way up through the crust but doesn't break through. The magma gets stuck

What makes the tides?

Even though the moon seems very far away, it really isn't all that far in scientific terms. In fact, it's close enough to exert a measurable force of gravity on everything on the Earth.

Water in the oceans is attracted by the moon's gravity. The pull of the moon causes the surface of the oceans facing the moon to mound up and push out in the direction of the moon. On the opposite side of the Earth, away from the moon, the same thing is happening, because of the force created by the Earth's rotation. The places where the oceans are mounding up the most are where there are high tides. These happen usually twice a day.

The sun also has some gravitational pull, but we don't usually notice it because it's not as strong as the moon's. But when the moon and the sun are in alignment, we get higher high tides and lower low tides, which are called spring tide. (Just because they're called spring tides doesn't mean they happen only in the springtime—they can take place all year round.) When the moon and the sun are working against each other, we get neap tides, lower high tides and higher low tides.

The moon's gravitational pull also works on the surface of the Earth. The crust is not completely stiff, and it mounds up, too. It raises only a few inches, and you never even notice it.

just under the surface of the crust, kind of like a pimple that never bursts (if it bursts, then it's a volcano, which is a whole other story, but it is true that volcanoes can create mountains, too). When the stuck magma cools, its stays put, forming a dome-shaped mountain.

But not all mountains are formed by the movement of the plates. Some mountains are erosion mountains, or plateau mountains. Plateaus are large flat areas at least 900 feet (274 m) above sea level. These get their shape by erosion—the name given to the process when wind or water wears rock away over millions of years. New Zealand's mountains are erosion mountains.

🔬 Discover this!

There are more mountains under the oceans than there are on land! This is because most plate boundaries are found under the oceans. Many islands are the highest peaks of mountains rising out of the water.

World's tallest mountains

Name	Mountain range	Elevation
Mount Everest	Himalayas	29,029 ft. / 8,848 m
Kilimanjaro	Karakoram	28,251 ft. / 8,611 m
Kangchenjuga	Himalayas	28,169 ft. / 8.586 m
Lhotse	Himalayas	27,940 ft. / 8,516 m
Makaly	Himalayas	27,838 ft. / 8,485 m

Tallest mountains in North America

Name	Mountain range	Elevation
Mount McKinley	Alaska	20,320 ft. / 6,194 m
Mount Logan	Yukon, Canada	19,541 ft. / 5,956 m
Pico de Orizaba	Veracruz, Mexico	18,491 ft. / 5,636 m
Mount Saint Elias	Alaska/Yukon	18,008 ft. / 5,489 m
Volcán Popocatépetl	Pueba, Mexico	17,749 ft. / 5,410 m

EARTHQUAKE!

Sometimes the change on Earth created by the movement of plates isn't slow and steady. Sometimes it's pretty dramatic and terrifying. Earthquakes are one example of plates moving around with pretty amazing results.

Earthquakes happen at places where two plates are sliding past each other. But they're not sliding smoothly—instead, they're rubbing and pushing and causing a lot of stress and strain on the crust, which sometimes cracks. These cracks are called **faults,** and many earthquakes happen along fault lines. One of the most famous faults in the U.S. is the San

The Ring of Fire

More than 80 percent of all earthquakes and more than half of all volcanoes happen along the Ring of Fire, a very long fault line that passes by Japan, India, and the Philippines, past China, up to Alaska, and then down along the West Coast of the United States. The San Andreas Fault is part of the Ring of Fire. Most of the time these earthquakes take place in the Pacific Ocean, and only those scientists who study earth- quakes notice. But other earthquakes, such as the one that hit Japan in 2011, are very dangerous.

Andreas Fault, which runs along the coast in California for more than 560 miles (900 km).

Earthquakes can take place anywhere two plates are moving past each other. Sometimes the plates just get stuck against each other for a while. When they finally get moving, it's with a shudder or a bang (actually an earthquake). The energy is released in seismic waves that travel up toward the surface of the Earth, where they're felt as vibrations. Sometimes the vibrations are so small that you don't even notice them. Other times they can be strong enough to knock down buildings and create massive destruction.

The volcanic island

If there were not volcanoes, there would be no Hawaii today. The island of Hawaii is made up of five volcanoes. One of them, Mauna Loa, is the world's largest active volcano. It takes up more than half the big island of Hawaii. Its name in Hawaiian means "long mountain," which is a good description because it's around 30 miles wide and 60 miles (48 x 97 km) long. It's 13,677 feet (4,169 m) high. If you measure it from its base under the Pacific Ocean, it's even taller than Mount Everest, the highest mountain in the world.

Scientists think Mauna Loa has been erupting for more than 100,000 years. The last time was in 1984. And it's not the only active volcano on Hawaii: Kilauea is also active—it hasn't stopped erupting since 1983, and millions of tourists visit it every year. Its name in Hawaiian means "spewing," and that's a good description, too. The eruptions that have been happening since 1984 aren't explosive. The lava is pouring slowly down the side of the mountain, and it has extended the island even farther into the sea.

MOLTEN MOUNTAINS

Earthquakes are not the only danger near fault lines. Volcanoes are also more likely to occur near fault lines than anywhere else in the world. Volcanoes are places, usually mountains, where magma spews out of the crust and up onto the surface of the Earth. Magma rises to the surface because it is less dense then the solid rock is the crust. As it starts to rise up through a crack in the crust, dissolved gases within it push it up faster and harder. It moves faster and faster as it gets closer to the surface of the Earth, finally exploding out. Once magma escapes onto the surface of the Earth, it is called **lava.**

There are more than 1,500 active volcanoes in the world. An active volcano is one that scientists think could erupt at any time. Volcanoes that haven't erupted for a while but might erupt are called **dormant.** Extinct volcanoes are ones that haven't erupted in a really long time and probably won't ever erupt ever again.

Mount Vesuvius—he was there!

In the year 79 Mount Vesuvius, near modern-day Naples, erupted explosively, burying the towns of Herculeum and Pompeii and killing up to 20,000 people.

This region of ancient Rome was very prosperous. All along the sides of the mountain, vineyards and gardens thrived in rich soil. The towns were beautiful, with many homes decorated with beautiful murals. The people living there had no idea that they were residing next to a time bomb—the volcano had not erupted for at least 2,000 years. There was a warning in the year 63, when an earthquake hit the city that knocked down several houses, but nobody thought much of it.

Then on the morning of 79, the eruption was witnessed by two famous Roman writers: Pliny the Elder, a general in the Roman navy and a scientist who wrote a 37-volume science encyclopedia, and his nephew, Pliny the Younger.

The two men witnessed an enormous cloud rising over the mountains, and they described it like a giant pine tree, "because it rose to a great height on a sort of trunk and then split off into branches."

Pliny the Elder immediately ordered his naval fleet to sail toward the cloud, knowing that people would need to be rescued. He invited his nephew to join him, but the young man said no, preferring to stay home and study. As he got close to the shore, Pliny the Elder found that his way was blocked: "Ashes were already falling, hotter and thicker as the ships drew near, followed by bits of pumice and blackened stones, charred and cracked by the flames: then suddenly they were in shallow water, and the shore was blocked by the debris from the mountain."

Eventually, the ships landed in the town of Stabiae. There he saw fires raging on the mountain. Buildings were being filled with ashes and volcanic pumice stones, and violent tremors were shaking the town. Although it was daytime, "they were still in darkness, blacker and denser than any ordinary night" as the mountain spewed out tons of lava, ash, poisonous gas, and stones.

The eruption of Vesuvius lasted six days. The ash and mud that fell onto the towns was turned to mud and then concrete by the rain that followed, and Pompeii and Herculaneum were not found by archaeologists until 1748. Among the 20,000 people who died there was Pliny the Elder, who bravely stayed around to help others escape. Today scientists call volcanic eruptions that send big plumes of gas and ash into the air **Plinian eruptions** after the scientist who observed this one so close up.

CURRENT EVENTS

The oceans cover more than 70 percent of the Earth's surface, yet so much about them remains a mystery to scientists. Undersea explorers find new species of fish and new geological features all the time.

Under the oceans, you'll find some of the deepest valleys and the highest mountains in the world. In fact, the longest mountain range in the world is one we never see. It is called the Mid-Atlantic Ridge, and it stretches for around 7,000 miles (11,265 km) under the Atlantic Ocean. The mountains in this range were all formed by the eruptions of undersea volcanoes.

There is much scientists don't know about life under the oceans, but they do know a lot about how the oceans affect our lives on land. It turns out that the oceans have a lot to do with controlling the weather.

The oceans are constantly moving. Of course, anyone who has been swimming at the beach could tell you that after getting thrown about by the waves. But there are some ocean movements that are even bigger than the tide.

There are regular movements—called **currents** of warm and cold water swishing all around the oceans. Some currents move warm water from the equator and other hotter parts of the planet toward freezing cold North and South poles. Other currents take cold arctic and Antarctic water from the poles and move it down toward the hotter places on Earth. The warm water heats the air above it as it flows, and the cool water cools the air above it. These ocean currents help to balance the temperature around the planet. Otherwise, it would be baking hot in the warmer parts of the Earth, like near the equator, and even more freezing cold in the cold parts, like near the North and South Pole.

The Arctic Ocean is the coldest ocean on Earth. There, water temperatures all year remain below 32°F (0°C). Water usually freezes at this temperature, but because ocean water is salty, it freezes at a lower temperature than fresh water. (The Southern Ocean, around Antarctica, varies from 28° to 50°F (-2°–10°C). The Indian Ocean is the warmest—and also the saltiest! The average water temperature there is roughly 65°F (18.5°C)!

The deepest of the deep

The deepest point in the oceans is called Challenger Deep. It's in the Mariana Trench, in the Pacific Ocean At its lowest point, it is 35,840 feet (10,925 meters) deep. That's almost seven miles! The Mariana Trench is a place where two platess meet. The Pacific Plate, the biggest plate in the Earth's crust, is wedged underneath the smaller Mariana Plate. Scientists have made it down to the bottom of the Mariana Trench only three times. But even though it's so deep, they found flounder and shrimp living down there!

EXPERIMENT

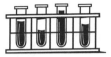

CLOUD IN A BOTTLE

What is the difference between a cloud, fog, and steam? They are all made of water and look whitish. You know that steam is hot, unlike fog, and this is because steam is water vapor—water in its state is a gas. In this state, water has the most energy, and its molecules are moving around the fastest.

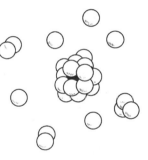

You already know how to make steam by heating water, but how do you make clouds and fog? Can you just cool off some steam with ice cubes?

Clouds form in the air when warm air rises. The higher it goes, the lower the air pressure. If the air has water vapor in it, the lower air pressure causes the water vapor to turn from gas to liqud. To make droplets, the water molecules need something to help them stick together. Particles,

continued ➡

like pollen, dust, or smoke, help water molecules group together. These are known as **condensation nuclei.**

You can experiment with cloud formation in a bottle. You will need to create a pressure change, condensation nuclei, and water vapor. You need to use matches in this experiment, so ask an adult to help.

Materials

- Clean 2-liter plastic bottle
- Warm water
- Long matches

Procedure

1. Fill a 2-liter bottle about $1/3$ to $1/2$ full with hot water from the tap and screw the cap on.

2. Squeeze the bottle to increase the pressure inside it, then release to decrease the pressure. Water might condense on the sides of the bottle, but you won't see anything resembling clouds or fog. Why not? What's missing?

3. Take the cap off.

4. Ask an adult to light a long match, then blow it out. (If you only have short matches, use them or a candle to light something long, like a stick of cardboard or a twig.) Your aim is to generate smoke in the bottle. Put the match into the bottle. You can let it fall in. Immediately put the cap back on to trap the smoke.

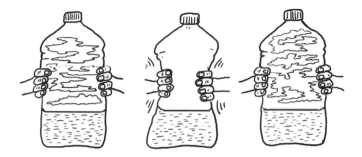

5. Squeeze the bottle and release it to lower the pressure. Do you see it fog up? That's a cloud!

6. Squeeze the bottle again. Does the cloud go away?

7. Squeeze the bottle again and open the cap to release the cloud. Can you feel it if you put your hand near the top of the bottle? Does it feel wet or cool?

8. Try making the cloud with more smoke. Have an adult place a few matches in the bottle. Do you get more cloud? What about using different temperatures of water or different amounts of water? Can you make a colored cloud by adding food coloring to the bottle?

Reader's Digest Books for Young Readers

I Wish I Knew That: Science

Why does matter matter? What makes the earth quake? How did life come about? Why does the moon shine? Kids will learn the answers to these and hundreds of fascinating questions about humans, earth, space, weather and climate, chemistry and so much more!

STEPHANIE SCHWARTZ DRIVER/RACHEL GARCIA
978-1-60652-424-4

I Wish I Knew That: U.S. Presidents

Starting with who is qualified to be president, what a president does, and how the president works with the rest of the government, this book, written just for kids, quickly turns to the fascinating profiles of each of the 43 presidents. There are also sidebars filled with fun and unusual information about our leaders.

PATRICIA A. HALBERT
978-1-60652-360-5

i before e (except after c)
The Young Readers Edition

Full of hundreds of fascinating tidbits presented in a fun and accessible way, this lighthearted book offers kids many helpful mnemonics that make learning easy and fun.

SUSAN RANDOL
978-1-60652-348-3

I Wish I Knew That: Geography

Kids will learn the basics about the world's continents, countries, and capital cities and marvel at the planet's most extraordinary physical features—from the highest mountains to the deepest oceans.

JAMES DOYLE
978-1-60652-347-6

ALSO AVAILABLE
I Wish I Knew That 978-1-60652-340-7
Write (Or Is That "Right"?) Every Time 978-1-60652-341-4

Each book is $9.99 hardcover
For more information visit us at RDTradePublishing.com
E-book editions also available

Reader's Digest books can be purchased through retail and online bookstores. In the United States books are distributed by Penguin Group (USA), Inc. For more information or to order books, call 1-800-788-6262.